TWO PLAYS
by
HOWARD MOSS

Books by Howard Moss

POEMS
Notes from the Castle   1979
A Swim off the Rocks   1976
Buried City   1975
Selected Poems   1971
Second Nature   1968
Finding Them Lost   1965
A Winter Come, A Summer Gone   1960
A Swimmer in the Air   1957
The Toy Fair   1954
The Wound and the Weather   1946

CRITICISM
Writing Against Time   1969
The Magic Lantern of Marcel Proust   1962, 1979

EDITED, WITH AN INTRODUCTION
New York: Poems   1980
The Poet's Story   1973
The Nonsense Books of Edward Lear   1964
Keats   1959

SATIRE
Instant Lives   1974

TWO PLAYS
by
HOWARD MOSS

The Palace at 4 A.M.
The Folding Green

The Sheep Meadow Press/Flying Point Books
New York City

ISBN: 0-935296-12-3
Library of Congress catalog card number: 80-52196

Copyright © 1958, 1967, 1980 by Howard Moss. All rights reserved, including the right of reproduction in whole or in part in any form.

CAUTION: Professionals and amateurs are hereby warned that The Palace at 4 A.M. and The Folding Green are subject to a royalty. They are fully protected under the copyright laws of the United States of America, and of all countries covered by the International Copyright Union (including the Dominion of Canada and the rest of the British Commonwealth), and of all countries covered by the Pan-American Copyright Convention and the Universal Copyright Convention, and of all countries with which the United States has reciprocal copyright relations. All rights, including professional, amateur, motion picture, recitation, lecturing, public reading, radio broadcasting, television, and the rights of translation into foreign languages, are strictly reserved. Particular emphasis is laid upon the question of readings, permission for which must be secured from the author's agent in writing.

All inquiries concerning rights (other than amateur rights) should be addressed to the author's agent, Helen Merrill, 337 West 22nd Street, New York, N.Y. 10011, without whose permission in writing no performance of the plays may be made.

The amateur production rights of The Palace at 4 A.M. and The Folding Green are controlled exclusively by DRAMATISTS PLAY SERVICE, INC., 440 Park Avenue South, New York, N.Y. 10016. No amateur performance of either play may be given without obtaining in advance the written permission of the DRAMATISTS PLAY SERVICE, INC., and paying the requisite fee.

For EDWARD ALBEE

CONTENTS

THE PLACE AT 4 A.M.
1

THE FOLDING GREEN
57

THE PALACE AT 4 A.M.

THE PALACE AT 4 A.M. was first performed at the Playwrights Unit, Theatre Vandam, in New York City, on 25 April, 1968, in a staged reading, with the following cast:

                Queen   RUTH FORD
                Edward   PAUL ROEBLING
                Figure   PAUL SPARER

Director, Charles Gnys

THE PALACE AT 4 A.M. received its first professional production at the John Drew Theater, East Hampton, N.Y. on 9 August, 1972, with the following cast:

                Queen   BEATRICE STRAIGHT
                Edward   CHRISTOPHER WALKEN
                Figure   DEAN SANTORO

Director, Edward Albee
Scenic Designer, James Tilton
Production Stage Manager, Charles Kindl
Lighting, James Tilton

CHARACTERS

QUEEN, *between forty-five and fifty*
EDWARD, *in his early twenties*
FIGURE, *neither young nor old, say, in his forties, but of an athletic build, lithe*

ACT ONE

SCENE: *No definite time or place. A large room but, visibly, its function remains mysterious. A small platform, center and somewhat downstage, on which a chair is set. Now, it resembles a throne. Attached to its shoulders, there may be royal standards, or what appear to be. An invisible window at right stage. (Right and left are audience's right and left.) A door slightly to the left of throne in back wall, now closed, and so made that it is not clear whether the door is really there or not—in other words, it might be part of the wall. The audience should not be aware of its existence until it is used. A rectangular bench downstage right.*

AT RISE: *QUEEN sitting erect on throne. SHE is wearing a contemporary dress, simple, elegant, the sort of thing a woman might wear for traveling or to a cocktail party.*
To her left, EDWARD stands facing her. HE wears something to suggest a formality and elegance of no particular time. Perhaps jeans or white duck trousers, a Greek or Indian tunic, and sandals.
FIGURE is dressed in some sort of uniform; a chauffeur's jodhpurs and jacket would do. HE stands behind QUEEN. Her chair must hide his hands. HE is impassive, and is treated by QUEEN and EDWARD at first as if THEY were unaware of his existence.
The stage is brightly lit.

QUEEN *(Looking around)*: And this room...this is the...?
EDWARD: Playroom, you might say.

5

QUEEN: It's rather somber for a playroom. *(Pause)* And there are no children.

EDWARD *(Staring at her)*: No.

QUEEN: A playroom with no children. Odd.

EDWARD: There are houses with libraries—hundreds of them—in which no one ever reads.

QUEEN: Still, the books are there. There's always the possibility.

EDWARD: Children are always a possibility. *(Laughs, not pleasantly.)* They're not very hard to make. All it takes is a man and a woman.

QUEEN *(Ignores this.)*: There are no games—no seesaws. I mean . . . no ladders.

EDWARD *(Lightly)*: It's an ascetic playroom. A fun house for puritans.

QUEEN: That sounds dreary. For children—as well as everyone else.

EDWARD: What's dreary for children *is* dreary for everyone else. Or so *I've* always thought. [*THEY are silent.*] Are you comfortable?

QUEEN: No. I'm nervous. Are the doors locked?

EDWARD *(Puzzled)*: What doors?

QUEEN *(Irritated)*: The doors to the house, of course.

EDWARD: How should *I* know? This is *your* house.

QUEEN *(Astonished)*: *My* house! Edward—are you feeling all right?

EDWARD: I've felt better. And worse. I thought you knew where we were.

QUEEN *(Trying to get the facts straight)*: I walked here with you . . . past trees, past a fountain . . . I'm in a room . . . A playroom, according to you . . . Surely, *you* know . . .

EDWARD: I know at times . . . and then it slips away . . .

QUEEN *(Sociably now, to get on a safe level)*: I haven't the faintest. How could I? I'm surprised by the extent of the grounds, of course, and it all does seem terribly palatial.

EDWARD: Palatial—meaning palaces?

Act One

QUEEN: Elaborate . . . big . . . *(SHE looks around again.)* It *is* a remarkable re-creation.

EDWARD: Re-creation of what?

QUEEN: That's what I was going to ask you. I'm really not up on architectural periods.

EDWARD: Oh, stop it. You've been here before.

QUEEN: When?

EDWARD: Centuries ago.

QUEEN: I have *not* been here before. I know where I've been.

EDWARD: You're luckier than most. *(Now giving her the facts HE knows.)* We're in your house, not mine. And the word *house*, by the way is a bit modest . . . *(HE stops, not quite sure.)* Or is it *our* house?

QUEEN: You're talking in riddles.

EDWARD: Unless I'm absolutely crazy, we're in a palace in . . . in Troy? *(Stops, puzzled.)* No . . . Thebes.

QUEEN: Thebes! You *are* crazy!

EDWARD *(Slowly)*: I . . . wish . . . I . . . were.

QUEEN *(Very nervous)*: You're trying to frighten me.

EDWARD: I'm not. I know you're nervous. [*On his line, the murmur of a CROWD over loudspeakers, rising in volume, and coming to a crescendo. As the sound rises, FIGURE retires to the right side of the stage, near the footlights, and seats himself on the floor. The sound of the CROWD diminishes, and stops.*] I know you're nervous.

QUEEN *(Passing her hand in front of her forehead)*: Who wouldn't be? With that crowd outside . . . thousands of them, waiting. Waiting for the first false move. *(SHE puts her head in her hands.)* I can't . . .

EDWARD: Do you think I like going through with it, time after time? Not really quite knowing whether to do this . . . or that . . .

QUEEN: Make up your mind.

EDWARD: As if it were mine to make up!

QUEEN *(Leaning forward)*: I beg you not to do it. I beg

7

The Palace at 4 A.M.

you not to go through with it. There's still time, still hope . . .
    EDWARD: You talk like a child. You think it's *my* decision? It was taken out of my hands years ago.
    QUEEN: I don't want to know the whole story. I swear I could stop now, retire . . . .
    EDWARD: Retire to where?
    QUEEN: Some small retreat, the two of us, another country . . .
    EDWARD: And what country do you think would have us?
    QUEEN: *Any* country! France, Chile, England . . . Believe me, Edward, there's still time. I know more than you do. Of what has been, of what's to come . . .
    EDWARD: Then *you* tell *me*.
    QUEEN: I have glimmerings, intuitions . . . *(SHE gets up, walks to imaginary window. Sounds of the crowd are heard.)* Listen to them! That hideous old man! When I think of my kindnesses, my favors . . . I treated him as one of our own. I lavished affection . . . [*EDWARD laughs.*] Yes, affection! When there was no meat, I gave him meat. When it snowed, I took him in.
    EDWARD: It snowed here? Here, by this hot sea?
    QUEEN: Once. A phenomenon. *(Back to her other thought.)* Beware of the blind!
    EDWARD: You went to bed with him . . .
    QUEEN: Never!
    EDWARD *(Impatiently)*: Not *him*! You know damn well who I mean.
    QUEEN: Oh! Naturally. I had to . . . Where would we all be?
    EDWARD: *We?*
    QUEEN: I was legally bound. It had nothing to do with natural affection. How many times do you have to be told, reassured . . . It gets boring . . . This endless repetition . . . You forget you're a King! As well as that . . . that . . . other thing.
    EDWARD: What other thing? If you know, say it.

Act One

QUEEN: I don't know. I have insights, gleanings. *(As if the subject dropped out of her mind.)* I would love a cup of coffee. Or maybe something stronger.
EDWARD: What do you want me to do?
QUEEN *(Imperiously)*: I *said* I'd love a cup of coffee.
EDWARD *(Irritated)*: I mean *really*. What do you want me to do? Make it clear—in one line.
QUEEN: DON'T DO IT! It's that simple.
EDWARD *(Slowly)*: Do *what*? I have just so much patience, just so much strength . . . I could kill . . .
QUEEN: And add another pearl to your string? Let's not threaten each other. It's *our* necks we're saving.
EDWARD: Ours? Or *yours*?
QUEEN: All right. I'll make it plain.
EDWARD: *Very* plain. No enigmas. No double talk. Who else did you sleep with?
QUEEN *(Angrily)*: You're impossible. You ask for one thing, you want another . . .
EDWARD: I'm sorry. Help me. We only have a few more hours . . . *(Pause)* Or centuries . . .
QUEEN: Which is it?
EDWARD: Hours that will seem like centuries.
QUEEN: Then think of something—something to kill time. We might as well kill it: it kills everyone else.
EDWARD: But we go on forever? Is that what you were going to say? Something cheap like that? You can be surprisingly cheap.
QUEEN: I was going to say something like that.
EDWARD: We'll play games. That'll pass the time.
QUEEN: Games? Such as?
EDWARD: You used to make up games for me when I was . . . when we were . . . whatever we were.
QUEEN: I can't remember any. I must be terribly old by now. Do I look terribly old?
EDWARD: Not terribly.
QUEEN: That's good.

The Palace at 4 A.M.

EDWARD *(Half maliciously, half truthfully)*: You don't look *young*.
QUEEN *(Pained)*: Ah . . . that's not so good!
EDWARD *(Back to games)*: So . . . what shall it be?
QUEEN: *You* start.
EDWARD *(Impulsively)*: Name every tree you know.
QUEEN *(Not annoyed, the lady dallying)*: Oh, *really*, Edward!
EDWARD: I mean it. If you examine *any* game, it's silly.
QUEEN: Pine, oak, gingko . . .
EDWARD: Good!
QUEEN: Ailanthus—the tree of heaven . . .
EDWARD: No digressions. A game of no digressions.
QUEEN: Aspen, beech, sassafras . . .
EDWARD: Good!
QUEEN: That's a digression.
EDWARD: Sorry.
QUEEN: Teak, birch, tamarisk . . .
EDWARD: That's *very* good.
QUEEN: Cherry, peach, plum . . .
EDWARD: That's not fair—going into the fruits.
QUEEN: They're trees, aren't they? So they're fair.
EDWARD: Well, then you can go into the nuts . . .
QUEEN: I'm sick of your game. I'd rather do nothing.
EDWARD: That is precisely what we will not be allowed to do. *(Pause)* All right. Another game: What did you do all day?
QUEEN *(Passing her hand before her forehead)*: I shopped. I had my hair done. I went for a walk in the park . . .
EDWARD: Alone?
QUEEN: Yes, alone. Completely. *(Pause)* You might even say terribly. Terribly alone.
EDWARD: Well, it's the human condition.
QUEEN: Is it? I wouldn't know. It seems we walked down a staircase and out of the human race.
EDWARD: I wouldn't say that. We're in it . . . and out of it.

Act One

QUEEN: I'd prefer to be one or the other.
EDWARD *(Pause)*: Do you ever think of me during the day? Do you ever miss me?
QUEEN *(Too casually)*: Of course.
EDWARD: I don't mean as a matter of course. I mean desperately. A sudden pang? As if there were a hole in space?
QUEEN: I *have* missed you that way.
EDWARD: I see. *(Not wanting to go on, but being forced to.)* Recently?
QUEEN: I think so.
EDWARD *(Hating himself, as if forced out of him)*: You *do* still love me?
QUEEN: In very much the same way I did.
EDWARD: Oh, but that means something's different, doesn't it?
QUEEN: Look: let's not go over it again and again. Let's change the whole subject. *(Pause)* Shall I tell you a dream I had?
EDWARD *(Bored)*: Go on. I'm listening.
QUEEN: I arrived in Cadiz. Parrots in cages. Remarkable black sand. I felt free, as if I walked in my own light. There were boats with blue sails, fish draped on the nets, the sun trapped in their scales. I became lighter, walked with a different tread. The grace of nature inspired me; the grass rose to my feet, grateful; the trees bent down to protect me. The sea shone at the sight of me. I felt nothing but pure energy, benign and certain. I had achieved some extraordinary pinnacle. I was alone and happy. I had been freed, not of death, but of love.
EDWARD: I would put that another way! You loved yourself for the first time.
QUEEN: Yes.
EDWARD: It was selfish.
QUEEN: No more than a tree is selfish, or a rock on a road, undaunted by what passes by.
EDWARD: And me: Did you think of me?

The Palace at 4 A.M.

QUEEN: How could I? I didn't even think of myself.
EDWARD: I would have thought of you.
QUEEN: In *my* dream.
EDWARD: No. In *mine*.
QUEEN: But you're not thinking of me *now*. You're not listening to me.
EDWARD: I see you. I want to touch you.
QUEEN: I am more than skin deep.
EDWARD *(Ironically)*: I haven't been freed of love.
QUEEN: You haven't been freed *to* love. You touch me to make sure you're there.
EDWARD: What other way? Do you think I still believe in mirrors? They'll reflect anything. I've seen somebody else's face running out of my mirror at the edges.
QUEEN *(Annoyed)*: I can't even tell you a dream without your appropriating it. I think *your* game is appropriating *me*. There must be some other.
EDWARD: Such as?
QUEEN: I don't know.
EDWARD: Well . . .
QUEEN: Well?
EDWARD: Shall we be witty?
QUEEN: That would be nice.
EDWARD: Brevity is the soul. Of wit, I mean.
QUEEN: That could have been briefer. *I* can be brief. As well as long-winded. *(With a gesture, as if beginning to demonstrate.)* All things to all men. *(Giving EDWARD a special look.)* And *boys*.
EDWARD *(Too casually)*: Oh, boys. I didn't know you went in for boys.
QUEEN: Certainly not girls. No matter what you've heard.
EDWARD *(During this speech, HE imitates the three famous monkeys.):* I hear nothing. *(Pause)* I say nothing. *(Pause)* I *see* nothing. [*THEY look at each other. Silence.*]
QUEEN: You hear all right.
EDWARD: But I don't believe everything I hear. Do you?

Act One

QUEEN: Hearing is believing. A blind man told me so.
EDWARD: Anyone I know?
QUEEN: Don't you mean "anyone I *knew*"?
EDWARD: I think *you* mean "anyone I'm *going* to know."
QUEEN: Nicely done. *(Claps her hands.)* Bravo.
EDWARD: And now. How about epigrams? The sport of kings. Or is it fools? Do *you* want to start?
QUEEN *(Sudden, girlish shyness)*: No. *You* start.
EDWARD *(Taking some time to think)*: Tragedy, tragedy... the Greeks made a play for it.
QUEEN: A mirror is a clock that needs no winding.
EDWARD: And death is a vacuum that abhors nature.
[*A VOICE, very low, over loudspeakers, a whispering voice, starts to repeat "Death is a vacuum that abhors nature," "Death is a vacuum that abhors nature," etc.*]
EDWARD *(Suddenly, perhaps hurling himself at her feet)*: I'm afraid! I'm terribly afraid!
QUEEN *(She touches his head.)*: Oh, darling, don't be. We've been through it so many times . . .
EDWARD: I stopped the carriage. I could see his face as clearly as I see yours, there were cries, strangled breathing . . .
QUEEN: Please . . . Edward . . .
EDWARD: I KILLED A MAN!
QUEEN: Stop it!
EDWARD: I murdered!
QUEEN *(Coaxing a patient)*: Look at me, Edward. [*HE does.*] It was some sort of dream, a nightmare . . .
EDWARD *(Wanting to believe her)*: I dreamt it?
QUEEN: Yes. And you will dream it again and again. Try to calm yourself.
EDWARD: I'm trying . . . to get past . . . around . . .
QUEEN: I know.
EDWARD: Hold me . . . don't let me go . . . *(HE gets on his knees. SHE manages to get onto bench and cradles his head in her lap.)*
QUEEN: It will be all right . . . finally. We will go through

The Palace at 4 A.M.

it and beyond it . . .
    EDWARD: I don't believe you. I want to believe you, but I can't . . .
    QUEEN: Trust me. There is no one else left to trust. [*HE gets up onto bench, sits next to her.*]
    EDWARD: I'm afraid of the dark, of what is there and what is not . . .
    QUEEN: My beloved . . . my darling . . . my child . . . *(SHE gathers him into her arms, HE curls up. SHE rocks him back and forth the way a mother would comfort a baby. Crooning effect.)* Sleep, Edward, sleep. Soon it will be light. *(SHE holds him, cradled in full view of the audience—a straight-on view. A tableau of this for, say, four seconds.)* [*Lights out.* QUEEN *and* EDWARD *stay on, semi-invisible.* FIGURE *rises and walks to the center of the stage.* HE *prances about a bit, nervous, too much energy. Does a knee bend maybe. A stretch. Then takes out a hand mirror and a comb.*]
    FIGURE *(To mirror)*: The same gorgeous number. If the Queen had any brains . . . *(To audience)*: You know, I should have had Edward's part. I'm a much better actor. But I get nervous when I read. I wasn't doing my best at the audition . . . so they didn't know how good I am. He's nothing compared to me. He's an ordinary, little, run-of-the-mill summer-stock-company hack. I've been trained. I've done Shakespeare, Chekhov, Shaw—the big boys. They wanted me for *Hamlet* in Montreal, but, just my luck, I came down with hepatitis. *(Pause. Slyly.)* She was a Greek, too. I'm not as crass as I seem. *(Slowly slipping into the palace servant, slowly becoming slavish.)* I have feelings . . . I observe things . . . Walking over to the palace, I looked down at the stones under my feet. Gradations of cement. Fine traceries of bird feet. Thousands of years of the human imprint. I never say what I know . . . [*EDWARD stirs, waking up.*] Oh! They're getting on with it. *(Smiles to audience.)* Which means, of course, that I'm getting off. *(HE exits.)*
    EDWARD *(Wakes, rubs his eyes, and slowly gets up)*: Delicious—what a delicious sleep!

Act One

QUEEN: It was very short . . .

EDWARD: But very deep. I seem to have gone far away . . . It was dark . . . it was lovely . . .

QUEEN: And you feel . . . better?

EDWARD: Oh, fine. Fine. *(Looking around)* Where are we?

QUEEN: The throneroom in Thebes. *(Angrily)* Must we greet each other each time as if we had never met? You know me twice over. It is amazing how the body tries to evade its fate. You can look up at the gallows . . . and still be hungry.

EDWARD: Not I. I have a very sensitive stomach.

QUEEN: You always did, even as a chi . . .

[*THEY stare at each other.*]

EDWARD: We *both* know.

QUEEN: We both do *not* know.

EDWARD: All right. We don't know. We're just two innocents doing a puzzle.

QUEEN: I mean . . . well, to be more honest . . . we know and we *don't* know.

EDWARD: You *are* a lovely evader. We know, we don't know, we nearly do, it's clear but it's not clear . . . it's all terribly interesting.

QUEEN: Don't take that tone, Edward. It's rather humiliating to me, if you don't mind my saying so. [*HE looks at her with contempt.*] I have feelings, you know; I'm as sensitive as you are.

EDWARD: Then I pity you.

QUEEN: Let's not pretend we haven't known each other a long time.

EDWARD *(Jokingly but in anger)*: As what?

QUEEN *(Getting off the hook)*: Historical characters . . . dramatic figures . . .

EDWARD: Oh, come *on!*

QUEEN: You married me.

EDWARD: Three famous words—equally at home in cartoons and high places. You were a Queen. One doesn't refuse a Queen.

The Palace at 4 A.M.

QUEEN: Are you trying to suggest you didn't want to? That you were coerced? It's untrue, and you know it is . . .
EDWARD: Yes. I wanted to. I was in love with you . . .
QUEEN: And now?
EDWARD: Everything changes.
QUEEN: I see. *(In a sudden fury)* Remember one thing: I was a Queen before you were a King! There was a King before you!
EDWARD *(Slowly)*: I could kill you!
QUEEN *(Laughing, note of hysteria)*: Why bother? Just wait, we don't have long to wait!
EDWARD: Thanks to you.
QUEEN: I was a Queen, not a god. Thank them! Thank the gods!
EDWARD *(Bowing, mocking)*: I thank them humbly. I bow to their superior wisdom.
QUEEN *(Switching)*: This is wrong of us, Edward. To fight, to be petty, to cheapen ourselves. We're in this room, this space. At least it is *our* space.
EDWARD: The same could be said of a coffin.
QUEEN: No. That would be *your* space, or *my* space. This is ours. It's a big room—by any standard.
EDWARD: Any trap is small. Palace or closet, what's the difference?
QUEEN: Are you talking of everyone's life?
EDWARD: I'm talking about my own! You trapped me . . .
QUEEN: I didn't know what I didn't know. I was reared to make princes. I moved by instinct. I opened my heart . . .
EDWARD: And legs.
QUEEN: That is how princes are made. I am not exempt from humanity.
EDWARD: No. But there's a price for that.
QUEEN: I didn't know it was going to be so high. I was willing to bargain.
EDWARD: I think the time for bargaining is over. And who is there left to bargain with? Gods who do not appear,

Act One

fates that slide away in the dark? Here one minute, gone the next?

QUEEN: Well, that is everyone's fate.

EDWARD: I'm not afraid of death. I'm afraid of *shame*.

QUEEN: Your death will cure you of it.

EDWARD: But there is memory—other people's memory.

QUEEN: You're a King. You talk like a slave. One can face the worst and still behave well. There are examples.

[*On "examples," FIGURE rises and walks behind QUEEN's throne. HE stands there throughout following speeches, his hands hidden by the throne.*]

EDWARD: I do not want to become an example.

QUEEN: You're too late—you already are one. You were preoccupied with your own little problems. Jealousy is a murderer. It kills three people.

EDWARD: I think it kills one, while two enjoy it.

QUEEN (*After a tiny pause for thought*): No. In the end, it kills three.

EDWARD (*Lightly, ironically, fending it off*): Well, *we're* still here.

QUEEN: Yes.

EDWARD: And you know me now?

QUEEN: I knew . . . I know . . . I will know.

EDWARD: You *knew* . . . everything from the beginning?

QUEEN: No. Not from the beginning . . . Not at the *beginning* . . .

EDWARD (*Looking at her closely*): Is that our story?

QUEEN (*After a pause*): You know the story. [*FIGURE slowly lifts his hands behind the throne. HE holds a crown which HE slowly places securely on her head.*] (*As if SHE were continuing another conversation.*) . . . and that was the summer of the flies. A season of vast devastation. Crops were ruined, the beaches despoiled. Animals writhed in agony, not able to cover themselves with nets and cloths. It was an unspeakable summer, the like of which had never been seen before, has never been seen since. It warned us of the plague

The Palace at 4 A.M.

to come. The sea writhed in unexpected skeins, the waves too heavy to break with their burden of flies. I praised the spider in my sleep, I who have always been afraid of them. I longed for the web-builders to come, to build a huge web over the city. The sound was incredible; a constant orchestra of wings. The tide became inaudible, the sound of people's voices, raised in horror, could hardly be heard for the beating of wings . . . It was the summer I learned the meaning of patience. It was the summer I began to believe in the gods . . . I longed for the plague rather than the warning. I began to long for my own death . . . *(Breaking off as abruptly as SHE began. To FIGURE)*: You, there! [*FIGURE looks up, turns his head toward her.*] Could you get the Queen a cup of coffee, the exhausted Queen a little nourishment? [*FIGURE stares at her and goes out.*] *(Drooping)* Edward, I'm very tired. You have no idea how tired I am. Almost beyond the point of caring . . . I have a very small amount of resilience left, of flexibility . . . Let's leave while we still can . . . There's money . . . There's transportation . . .

EDWARD: And the plague?

QUEEN: We're immune.

EDWARD: We're responsible for the sufferings of thousands of people, for their deaths . . . And you suggest running away. You *are* heartless.

QUEEN: Heartless? What isn't heartless? Staying is heartless, going is heartless. At least going is an *action* . . .

EDWARD: And never to know? How could we live with each other? With ourselves? [*FIGURE returns, carrying a small tray on which there is a cup.*]

FIGURE *(Shyly, tentatively)*: Your Majesty?

QUEEN: Approach me. Bring it to the throne. [*HE does. HE kneels before her and offers her the tray.*] I have never tasted untasted food. Where is the smaller cup so that I may offer you some?

FIGURE: It . . . broke. Forgive me. [*THEY look at each other.*]

Act One

QUEEN: Taste it first. [*FIGURE begins to tremble.*] What are you afraid of?

FIGURE *(Tries to control himself)*: I am afraid for my life, Madame.

QUEEN: You should be afraid of your death.

FIGURE: They mean the same thing, Madame.

QUEEN: I beg to differ. They *almost* mean the same thing.

FIGURE: Shall I take it from the tray? Am I permitted?

QUEEN *(Handing him cup)*: Taste it! [*FIGURE takes sip of coffee, hands it back to her.*] I will watch you for a minute. Slow poison is for kings.

EDWARD *(Bitterly)*: There are so many forms of slow poison.

QUEEN *(Not responding to EDWARD. Watching FIGURE closely. To FIGURE)*: Nothing is happening to you, is it?

FIGURE: No, Your Majesty.

QUEEN: You addressed me as "Madame" before. Why?

FIGURE: I beg your pardon, Your Majesty.

QUEEN *(Brightly, sociably, to EDWARD)*: It seems sometimes I'm secular and sometimes I'm sacred. And sometimes I'm royal and sometimes I'm common.

EDWARD: As befits a Queen who was not always a Queen.

QUEEN: A compliment from the King! *(To FIGURE)*: Have you ever desired to be royal? Tell the truth.

FIGURE: Only once, Madame.

QUEEN: Your Majesty. And when was that?

FIGURE: When I felt lust for a Queen.

[*QUEEN begins to sip coffee.*]

EDWARD *(Coming downstage, to FIGURE)*: You!

FIGURE: Yes?

EDWARD: What did you mean by that last remark?

FIGURE: Nothing, Your Majesty.

EDWARD: When did you feel lust for the Queen?

FIGURE: I said *a* Queen, Your Majesty, not *the* Queen.

QUEEN: Yes, he did. I felt so *general*.

EDWARD *(Violently grabbing FIGURE'S arm)*: If I ever

The Palace at 4 A.M.

thought . . .
  FIGURE *(Frightened)*: I was only trying to amuse the Queen. I was attempting to be light—to pass the time.
  EDWARD: Where were you born?
  FIGURE: In Syria, sir.
  EDWARD: Syria? You don't look Syrian. What do you do?
  FIGURE *(Shocked)*: Why, sir, I am your fool!
  QUEEN *(Disgustedly)*: Oh, leave him alone. Let him go. You're being a fool.
  EDWARD *(To FIGURE)*: Get out of here!
  FIGURE: Yes, Your Majesty. *(HE starts out. Then turns back with a pained and surprised look.)* Oh! How could I have forgot? A gift from the people! *(To EDWARD)*: For the Queen! *(HE takes a necklace out of his pocket, shows it to her, and places it around her neck. SHE accepts it with the preening look of a vain woman. FIGURE looks at EDWARD to see if it's all right. Done fast with a certain arrogance toward QUEEN and a certain obsequiousness toward EDWARD, if both can be managed at once. That look a dog has when he knows he's doing something wrong and at the same time looks at his Master to see if this time he'll get away with it.)*
  QUEEN *(Singsong)*: Love-ly.
  [*EDWARD watches them carefully.*]
  FIGURE *(Standing back to ascertain effect)*: Splendid. [*SHE fingers it, trying various little rearrangements.*] That's a good girl.
  EDWARD *(Enraged)*: GET OUT!
  FIGURE *(One last dig before he's forced to exit, flung back, on way out)*: The committee asked me to say it was a gift to a leader, as *well* as a leader of fashion. *(HE moves to side.)*
  QUEEN: Well, thank the committee so much.
  EDWARD *(To FIGURE)*: Get out of here! Out! [*FIGURE exits.*] That bastard! *Bastard! (To QUEEN)*: What committee?
  QUEEN: Oh, who knows. The Sewer Workers of Greek

Act One

Street, perhaps . . .

EDWARD: I don't know why they'd give *you* a necklace. Nothing for *me*, I noticed.

QUEEN *(To placate but without the slightest credibility)*: Maybe they're still working on yours . . .

EDWARD *(Comes over, and fingers necklace for a moment)*: Perhaps it's from The Leper Fingerpainters . . . *(Big grin.)* Their work is . . . falling off.

QUEEN: You *would* say something horrible like that. I don't care who gave it to me, frankly, or why. I love jewels. Such lovely talismans against death! They make the ugly woman seem beautiful and the beautiful woman timeless. And what the ugly want is to be beautiful and what the beautiful want is to last forever.

EDWARD: And which are you?

QUEEN *(Since HE should know, SHE won't play the game)*: Me? Oh, I make no claims one way or the other. I'm just a friend of the people. *(But SHE knows where to hurt him.) Lots* of people, actually . . . now that I think of it . . . .

EDWARD *(Coming toward her, quiet but threatening)*: You know, if I ever thought you and that Fool . . .

QUEEN: That *would* be foolish . . . In fact, you're the only commoner I ever slept with . . .

EDWARD: Really? The Sphinx didn't find me so common . . .

QUEEN *(Very airy and offhand)*: I don't count sleeping with freaks . . .

EDWARD: She could have taught you a thing or two . . . Besides, I did it for my country.

QUEEN: Corinth?

EDWARD: Thebes.

QUEEN: Oh! I thought you came from Corinth.

EDWARD: Oh, come on.

QUEEN *(SHE knows it all too well)*: It's *such* a tangled history . . . *(To EDWARD, in regard to FIGURE)*: Has he gone?

EDWARD: Yes.
QUEEN: You didn't think I could talk in front of him, did you? *(Furiously) Did* you?
EDWARD: I don't know. I don't know anything anymore. What is it you want me to do?
QUEEN: Stop asking questions. And then you won't stumble on *the* question. The border's only twenty miles from here . . . Edward, are you listening?
EDWARD: But what did I do? Tell me that. What did I do wrong?
QUEEN: Nothing. You have nothing to blame yourself for.
EDWARD: Was it better with him . . . than with me? Did you enjoy . . . ?
QUEEN: Stop it! Our lives depend on what we do in the next hour, and you . . .
EDWARD: Do it alone. I'm not going. Unless you tell me.
QUEEN: Yes. I went to bed with him, and . . . *(SHE stops.)*
EDWARD *(Grabbing her arm)*: And . . .and? And how many others?
QUEEN: There were several others. None of them important. I can hardly remember them . . .
EDWARD: Hardly! But there they are, between us, every time we go to bed!
QUEEN: No, no . . . With you . . . I've never been unfaithful . . . You know it . . . [*A yell, the sound of a CROWD, heard through the window. Then the distinct words "Edward, Edward, The King, The King."*] Go to the window, quickly. Please. [*HE goes to the window, waves. A rock is hurled through it. HE steps back.*] Those animals! Are you all right?
EDWARD: I think so . . . Yes.
QUEEN: I hope whoever threw it dies of the plague, of convulsions . . . Where's the key?
EDWARD: I don't have the key. Don't you have it?
QUEEN: Wait! [*SHE searches through her pockets, opens*

Act One

a purse, searches.] God, where is it? [*Hands purse to him.*] Look. It has to be somewhere.
   EDWARD: You always kept the keys. All the throne-room keys.
   QUEEN *(Extracting key from purse in his hands. SHE imitates the action of inserting key into imaginary lock in door behind throne. Pushes. Nothing happens.)* [*Shouts from outside: "The King, the King."*] Help me, for God's sake.
   EDWARD *(Pushing against door, trying various stratagems)*: It won't budge.
   QUEEN: It *has* to.
   EDWARD *(Exerting all his strength)*: It won't move an inch. It seems to be sealed.
   QUEEN: Impossible! *(SHE tries.)* [*They exert their strength together.*] *(Bitterly)* I wish the *King* were alive!
   EDWARD *(Stops abruptly, looks at her)*: I'm not going
   QUEEN: I'm very sorry I said that. I was thinking how strong he was. That's all. It was factual, not emotional.
   EDWARD: How you'd still like him to take you!—You still want him! Those rumors of a child! What about *them?*
   QUEEN: Rumors! There are a thousand rumors. Haven't you heard any about yourself? I have. How you swam eight miles in less than an hour. That you are a sadist. That you are dying of an obscure liver ailment. That you are a homosexual. That you have had a secret house built on Samothrace . . .
   EDWARD: You would know if you had a child.
   QUEEN: Yes. Who better? I did not have a child. Are you satisfied?
   EDWARD: No. *(Bitterly)* I don't believe you. How can I? Half of what you say contradicts the other half. Warnings. Hints. Clues. You know why I'm not reassured? Because there's no reassurance. If something happened, it happened; if something didn't, it didn't. All I ask is the truth. How many men did you sleep with?
   QUEEN: I don't know. There *is* no truth. Feelings about the truth, yes. Suppose I said I slept with ten men, or eighty-

The Palace at 4 A.M.

four. What difference would it make? Supposing nine meant nothing, and eighty-four a great deal. Or that none meant a damn thing. It's not the act, it's the meaning of the act. You should know that, you who are always probing, prying, trying to find the chemical formula for a piece of dust. I'm telling you the truth; I don't know! I DON'T KNOW!
    EDWARD: I'm sorry. I can't help it. It comes over me, stronger than anything, stronger sometimes than my love for you . . .
    QUEEN: If you love me, save me . . . and save yourself. There has to be *some*one to love!
    EDWARD: My people love me!
    QUEEN *(Looking at him incredulously)*: Didn't you feel that rock go past your face? The little wind it made was the distance between your skin and . . . Nothing!
    EDWARD: They *love* me.
    QUEEN: They love themselves more. Tiresias, the blind man is luring them away. But he needs your help. Don't help him!
    EDWARD: You know the border is closed.
    QUEEN: No border is closed. There are streams, a foot or two of undefended scrub, a small hill beyond the sentry guard, a hill nobody's ever noticed.
    EDWARD *(Pointing to window)*: I'm supposed to be *down* there with Tiresias. I'm supposed to ask him a question.
    QUEEN: Don't ask it. That's what I beg of you. Help me through the door.
    EDWARD: I don't believe there is a door there. This whole room may be a room in your imagination.
    QUEEN: The door is real. Just wait. They'll be in here with the usual torches, spears, maces—the whole royal paraphernalia of killing. You want to meet them? Do. I don't. Besides, if I were to imagine a room I can assure you it wouldn't be this one. *(Indicating window)* With *them* watching. *(Indicating audience)* And *them.* Why should I be used to satisfy their filthy fantasies?

Act One

EDWARD: Everyone satisfies someone else's fantasy. Why should *you* be exempt?

QUEEN: I *am* a Queen. After *all*. And I have my own life to lead—a dirty reality in itself.

EDWARD: Reality! I touch myself and I'm real. I look at you and I'm not sure.

QUEEN: Well then, perhaps you should leave me. I'll wait here alone. Quietly. Patiently. The knot will tie itself in the end. Never fear.

EDWARD: And while you're waiting, would you be alone? He *looked* at you. In a special way. He *stared* . . .

QUEEN: Who?

EDWARD: Our fool, our scarecrow, our phantom—the bringer of coffee!

QUEEN: STOP CROSS-EXAMINING ME!

EDWARD: Someday, I'll pay you back for treating me this way. For your condescension . . .

QUEEN: You threaten me? I, who gave you life? *(SHE stops, aghast. THEY both stare at each other.)*

EDWARD *(Incredulously)*: You didn't . . . You aren't! *(HE goes up to her, grabs her by the arm.)* Say you aren't! Say it!

QUEEN: I'm . . . I'm what? I don't know . . . [*HE begins to twist her arm.*] Edward!

EDWARD: Say "I am not your mother!" *Say it!*

QUEEN *(Very frightened)*: No, no, of course not. I was . . . joking.

EDWARD *(Letting go)*: It's part of your plan to confuse me, isn't it? To throw me off the track. [*SHE turns away. HE grabs her arm.*] Look at me! Answer me! When you finished with him, where did you go?

QUEEN: I ran out of the palace . . . I was beside myself . . . I realized they'd taken . . . I can't remember what! Something I wanted, something that belonged to me. It was unnatural what they were doing, it was cruel beyond anything I'd ever imagined . . . I remember staring at a river and looking up at the sky. Nothing mattered. I heard flies being born,

The Palace at 4 A.M.

saw strange wings, shadows over the landscape, and I ran back to the palace, which suddenly was full of birds, birds and their shadows on the ceiling. I pushed my head into the pillow not to scream . . .
    EDWARD: And he? Where was he?
    QUEEN: It's hard to remember, Edward. They drugged me, I'm sure. After that, there were days . . . maybe weeks . . . when I couldn't think, when every image was blurred . . .
    EDWARD *(Quietly)*: Why did you say it?
    QUEEN: What?
    EDWARD: That thing . . . that monstrous thing.
    QUEEN *(Now SHE is lying)*: I told you. I was joking. It came into my head and I said it.
    EDWARD: It's pain, all pain—that's what you came to bring me. Insidious forms of torture, telling me and not telling me, luring me on only to turn me away in the end. Is that it? Is that why you came? [*HE slaps her very hard across the face. SHE begins to cry.*]
    QUEEN: Oh, Edward.
    EDWARD *(Placing one hand in front of him)*: My hand is burning! *(HE kneels before her.)* I'm sorry. Forgive me. Please! I didn't know what I was doing. I swear. Please say you forgive me. Please!
    QUEEN: I forgive you, Edward. I can't change the past. Let me pretend there is a future. I don't want to go through with it to the bitter end!
    EDWARD: And you forgive me?
    QUEEN: I forgive you.
    EDWARD: I didn't mean it. I know you're afraid. I don't want to make you more afraid.
    QUEEN: Yes, I'm afraid. Of blind men . . .
    EDWARD: Swear to me—swear to me that no one else means anything to you.
    QUEEN: No one. I swear it. If we fall out, if we panic, no one will save us. Guards, soothsayers, doctors . . . Edward, listen to me carefully: Unless we act soon, we are both doomed.

Act One

EDWARD: Tell me the truth.
QUEEN: I can only tell you what I know!
EDWARD: But what you know seems to change from minute to minute, as if you were hiding something. *That* is what is so maddening. Put yourself in my place.
QUEEN: Oh, I try. You don't know how I try!
EDWARD: I'm sorry I said what I said. I love you. You know that.
QUEEN: If you love me, if you have *ever* loved me, HELP ME FIND THE KEY!
EDWARD: I will, I will. Let me look. [*SHE hands him her purse. HE looks through it, extracting a small photograph.*] This picture. Why do you have this picture?
QUEEN: Let me see. [*HE shows it to her.*] I don't know who it is.
EDWARD: Why do you lie to me? Why?
QUEEN *(Wearily)*: I am not lying. *(SHE goes back to throne, sits down.)* Edward, at the beginning I had half a hope. Now, I only have half of that . . .
EDWARD: I'll do anything you say—anything—if you'll tell me. Who is this man?
QUEEN: All right. I'll tell you. He is the man you made up. He is the man you wanted to find. He is the man you spawned in my purse.
EDWARD: What magical powers you give me . . . You're trying my patience. You're going too far!
QUEEN: I have never understood that phrase. One goes as far . . . *(SHE clutches at her neck, making a strangling sound.)*
EDWARD: What is it? What's the matter?
QUEEN: I'm . . . choking . . . *(SHE takes necklace from her neck, shows it to him.)* It seemed to wrap itself around me, tighter and tighter . . . *(SHE throws it on the floor; HE bends to pick it up.)*
EDWARD: You've never seen it before?
[*THEY stare at each other.*]

QUEEN: I have never seen it. *Never.*
EDWARD: You don't remember.
QUEEN: I would remember.
EDWARD: Look at the design! It's made of many keys. *(HE shows it to her.)*
QUEEN *(Handing it back)*: Are your . . . are your eyes . . . all right?
EDWARD: My eyes?
QUEEN: Yes.
[*Lights go slightly lower.*]
EDWARD: They're perfectly all right. Why?
QUEEN *(Evasively)*: I just wondered . . .
EDWARD: Is it getting darker?
QUEEN *(Very gently)*: Ever so slightly darker. [*Shouts again through the window: "Edward, the King, the King!"*] Eventually you will have to go down. Or we will have to leave through that door.
EDWARD *(Avoiding the choice, childishly)*: Could the key be anywhere else? Could you have . . . swallowed it? I know that sounds absurd.
QUEEN *(A certain grim humor)*: No. I don't eat keys, Edward.
EDWARD: I mean in your anxiety to hide it . . . [*The door slowly opens of itself. Light behind door.*] Look! We'll be saved!
QUEEN: If *we* opened it, Edward. *We!*
EDWARD: It must have swung open . . . the wind . . .
QUEEN: It is a very still day. It is the stillest day I ever remember.
EDWARD: There's some rational explanation, some physical law . . .
QUEEN *(As if talking to herself)*: Many strange and passing wonders. Help me to my feet, Edward. I'm very tired. I've come a long way . . .
EDWARD *(Going to her)*: Here, take my arm . . . steady . . . [*THEY stagger slightly, then stand facing the door.*]

Act One

QUEEN: I wonder if we will be . . . missed. Not *sought* after. Missed.

EDWARD: By whom? Who is left to care?

QUEEN: I have awakened in the middle of the night and felt that . . . if I died, if I simply did not appear—appear *forever*—who would care? And I have felt something worse, much worse . . .

EDWARD *(Drops her arm.)*: Are you thinking of your old lovers? Is that it?

QUEEN *(Going on with her own thoughts)*: That *I* wouldn't care! That I wasn't even *there* to care! I had gone away . . . I had become something else . . .

EDWARD: Tell me. Whom are you thinking of? Tell me! Before we do it!

QUEEN: And after we do it, and while we do it, and again and again and again . . .

EDWARD: I'm sorry. It . . . I don't know what happens.

QUEEN *(Turning on him, abruptly)*: Stop feeling guilty! Stop enjoying the guilt! It's disgusting.

EDWARD: I see. You have no pity for me. Only for yourself.

QUEEN: I pity myself—that's true. I have too much respect for you, too much love, to pity you. I endure myself. I hope for something better for you.

EDWARD: Let us go through the door, then. If you love me, let us go through the door . . .

QUEEN: Yes.

EDWARD: Shall I take the necklace?

QUEEN: Leave it here. I will come back to it. Or it will come back to me. *(As if SHE had a sudden thought, SHE goes to the empty cup left on the throne, looks at it, and throws it across the room. SHE screams.)*

EDWARD: What are you doing? What is wrong with you?

QUEEN: Look in it, Edward! Look in it! [*HE does.*] It is full of flies! [*A buzzing noise of wings, louder and louder, then stopping abruptly.*]

EDWARD: I don't see them. Where?
QUEEN: Hundreds of them. Thousands. It's so horrible!
(SHE hides her head in her hands.)
EDWARD: You're ill. It was something in the coffee . . . a drug . . .
QUEEN *(Getting calmer, resigned)*: No. No.
EDWARD: I'll take care of you . . . I've never loved anyone as much . . . Never!
QUEEN: Let us go, Edward.
EDWARD: Say it! Say it back!
QUEEN *(Confusedly)*: Say what?
EDWARD: Say you love me!
QUEEN: I *have* said it. I *just* said it.
EDWARD: Do you love me *now?*
QUEEN: Yes, I do. Yes.
EDWARD: Then hold me, kiss me . . .
QUEEN: Wait, Edward. Please. Give us a chance. Let us get through the door!
EDWARD: Just once, one little bit . . .
QUEEN: Edward, be very careful. Everything hangs in the balance. *(SHE allows him to embrace her. HE is passionate, SHE unresisting, passive.)*
EDWARD: My darling, I can't . . .
QUEEN: Edward!
EDWARD: I can't wait . . . I have to . . .
QUEEN: I beg you . . .
[*CROWD sounds again.*]
EDWARD: When I was a child . . .
QUEEN: Don't.
EDWARD: Your thighs, the small of your back . . . I feel them!
QUEEN *(Looking at him with some alarm)*: Edward . . . please.
EDWARD: I want you . . .
QUEEN: No, Edward . . . let me get ready . . .
EDWARD: Aren't you ready?

Act One

QUEEN: No. This gown is so wrinkled . . . my hair . . .

EDWARD: Oh, come on. You've been getting ready for centuries. Why hesitate at the last minute?

QUEEN *(Fending him off, a light tone that isn't convincing)*: Well, I'm a woman of some style, Edward. Don't think it's easy to appear superbly groomed as if it were perfectly natural. It takes hours of meticulous preparation . . . Color, tools . . .

EDWARD: You look all right to me. In fact, you look *very* all right.

QUEEN: I'm an old lady. I'm old enough to be . . .

EDWARD: I've heard all that rot. *(Shyly but falsely)* Don't you like me? Don't you think I'm attractive?

QUEEN: Oh, yes, very . . . but . . .

EDWARD: Come here and give your old dog a kiss.

QUEEN: No, Edward.

EDWARD: A little kiss for old time's sake?

QUEEN *(SHE begins to move away as HE moves closer)*: Edward . . . there's still time to avoid . . .

EDWARD: The unavoidable?

QUEEN: The door's still there. Look!

EDWARD: The hell with the door!

QUEEN *(Alarmed)*: Then think of the necklace, think of my neck!

EDWARD: I am thinking of it. It's a lovely neck.

QUEEN *(Now frightened)*: Edward, don't go through with it. Don't!

EDWARD: I'm tired of your restrictions, your prohibitions. I'm tired of being told what to do. I'm a man. *(Going after her)* Let me touch you . . . don't resist me . . .

QUEEN: For your *mother's* sake.

EDWARD: She's dead.

QUEEN: For your *wife's* sake.

EDWARD: I'm not going to listen . . . *(HE grabs her arm.)*

QUEEN: No! Please, Edward. Please. [*HE holds her*

closer, as SHE resists.]
 EDWARD: I've wanted this . . . for ages and ages . . .
 QUEEN *(Desperately)*: I'll tell you the whole story . . .
 EDWARD: You're so lovely. Your skin . . .
 QUEEN: Think of *them*, think of *them* down there . . .
 EDWARD: It's maddening . . . how I love you! [*SHE breaks away, HE follows and holds her.*]
 QUEEN: We'll be tangled in a net . . .
 EDWARD: We are! Let's enjoy it!
 QUEEN: No, no! [*HE forces her to bench.*]
 EDWARD: You're hot. I can feel it. Your breasts, your eyes . . .
 QUEEN: No!
 EDWARD: You want me! I know you do! *(HE forces her down onto the bench.)*
 QUEEN: You'll kill me!
 EDWARD: Kiss me . . . kiss me back . . .
 QUEEN: No, Edward, please, no.
 EDWARD *(HE puts his leg between hers, HE begins to try to take off her clothes)*: How I want you!
 QUEEN *(Rising voice, ending in sobs)*: No, Edward, please. I beg you . . . [*The door slowly closes.*] I beg you . . . I beseech you . . . [*Sobs, suddenly transformed to tape recording of sobs, very loud over loudspeakers.*] No . . . no . . .

CURTAIN

ACT TWO

SCENE: *The same, though the throne and bench may be repositioned. The door must be visible to the audience for it is to serve a double function now—it is also to be used as a screen for projections.*

AT RISE: *EDWARD, in royal cloak, sits on the throne in semi-darkness before the door-screen on which the image of the SPHINX is to be projected. The sound of buzzing flies is heard over the loudspeaker. The voice of the SPHINX throughout is that of FIGURE heard over a loudspeaker, sometimes menacing, sometimes cajoling, as the action demands.*

VOICE *(Softly but ominously, as the projection of the SPHINX appears)*: Sphinx, sphinx, sphinx, sphinx . . .

(EDWARD, as if responding to the sound, lies down on the bench in a contorted position.)

VOICE *(FIGURE's voice, very high, mannered, and, if possible, as if it were coming from a great distance)*: All . . . of . . . Thebes . . . is . . . infertile . . . He . . . who . . . can . . . answer . . . the . . . riddle . . . of . . . the . . . Sphinx . . . will . . . make . . . Thebes . . . fertile . . . again.

EDWARD *(In a strangled, tense voice)*: I . . . can . . . *(Thrashing from side to side on the bench.)* I . . . can . . . *(Their voices remain the same throughout.)*

VOICE: Those who fail die and are consumed.

EDWARD: I know.

VOICE: Can you solve the riddle of the Sphinx?

EDWARD: I . . . can . . .

VOICE: If a young man left Corinth for Thebes, and killed his father on the way, what would his name be?

EDWARD: That . . . is . . . not . . . the . . . riddle.

VOICE: When is the Queen's husband the son of a whore?

EDWARD: That is not the riddle.

VOICE: When is the Queen's son the *husband* of a whore?

EDWARD: When . . . *(HE stops himself.)* That is not the riddle.
VOICE: Am I serpent, man, animal or bird?[1]
EDWARD: That is not the riddle.
VOICE: The lion longs for you, and the eagle, too. Come closer, sweet.
EDWARD: No . . . no . . .
VOICE: Kiss me—and we'll forego the riddle. Don't you like my hair?
EDWARD: That is not the riddle.
VOICE: Answer this, or die. Can you answer it?
EDWARD *(Groaning sound; HE tries to hide his head)*: Yes . . . *(Some light effect here?)*
VOICE: What being, with only one voice, has sometimes two feet, sometimes three, sometimes four, and is weakest when it has the most?
EDWARD: I . . . I . . . I . . . I . . .
VOICE: What? What?
EDWARD *(Making supreme effort)*: "Man! Because he crawls on all fours as an infant, stands firmly on his two feet in his youth, and leans upon a staff in his old age."
LOUDSPEAKER *(The sound of the crowd)*: The King! The King!
(Crowd sounds build to a loud roar. The image of the SPHINX fades. The stage goes absolutely dark, there is total silence. Lights up on EDWARD on throne. HE gets up and walks over to the imaginary window. HE looks down.)
EDWARD: They're not calling for me anymore. It's deathly still. I have never heard such a silence. There are nights like this, when the stars remove themselves to a great distance, when the moon seems to apologize for itself. When reflection and shadow meet and become each other. *(HE passes his hand in front of forehead.)* I have been some place where

---

[1] The traditional figure of the Sphinx has a woman's head, lion's body, serpent's tail, and eagle's wings.

Act Two

four roads cross . . . *(With gradually rising emotion.)* I have seen wheels churning upside-down in broad daylight, carriages going forward at noon, whose passengers suddenly arrive in the dark. We are all going to arrive at the same place! *(HE comes forward, closer to the footlights.)* We are in a museum together mounted, all, in glass cases. One day—which day?—a careless hand will reach out and break them. How? When? *(HE calms down.)*

FIGURE *(Enters downstage. EDWARD sits down on the throne. FIGURE at his feet.)*: Have you forgiven me?

EDWARD: I forgive you—as long as there is nothing to forgive.

FIGURE: I swear, Your Majesty. Nothing. *(HE looks at EDWARD for a moment.)* You look sad.

EDWARD: I am. I see nothing but the future's inescapability.

FIGURE: How will you pass the time?

EDWARD: Wretchedly.

FIGURE *(Slyly)*: And expensively. *(Indicating the audience.)* For *them*, I mean.

EDWARD: For all of us.

FIGURE *(Changing sides)*: They didn't come here just to watch you pass the time, you know. They *paid*.

EDWARD: I'm paying. *(Pause.)* What *did* they come for?

FIGURE: To be entertained. Amused. Perhaps moved. You *do* look sad. Try to think of something pleasant . . .

EDWARD: I'm open to suggestion.

FIGURE: Well, you're a King. No matter what happens, how many people could say as much?

EDWARD: You're a fool. Does that bring you comfort?

FIGURE *(Turning to audience)*: I am not . . . *always* . . . a fool.

EDWARD: Have the crowds dispersed?

FIGURE: No. They are still waiting.

EDWARD: And he?

FIGURE: Who?

EDWARD: The blind man.

FIGURE: He has stopped in the middle of telling a story. *(Imparting a confidence)*: He doesn't *want* to tell it, you know.

EDWARD: And I don't want to live it.

FIGURE: There *is* a way out: you could kill yourself. [*THEY look at each other.*]

EDWARD: Wouldn't *you* be disappointed?

FIGURE: Of course. And sorry, too, but I'm a special case . . . like you. I'm in it . . . and I'm out of it.

EDWARD: As a special case, then, I'd like to be left alone.

FIGURE: That's unkind.

EDWARD: Unkinder than you are?

FIGURE: I'm cruel and kind. Like everybody.

EDWARD: You're beginning to bore me.

FIGURE: Oh? Then why don't I become someone else? Artifice, guise, pretense . . . *(HE has picked up a gnarled cane.)* Being a Fool, I can play more roles than a King. *(HE says the last word with menace and emphasis.)* By the way, I should remind you. There are no guards to run forward with shields. There is no one to light the torches. *(On the word "torches," FIGURE puts on dark glasses and assumes the character of TIRESIAS.)*

EDWARD: I hope the story you're telling down in the courtyard is an interesting one . . .

FIGURE: It isn't an amusing story. But then, I've been away from *brilliant* society for so long that perhaps I've lost touch.

EDWARD: That's something the blind should never do—lose touch.

FIGURE *(Turning his head toward EDWARD)*: If you asked me here to tell me what I know . . .

EDWARD: It's just the other way around—to tell *me* what you know. What does your story mean?

FIGURE: It isn't finished, so I'm not certain. So far, it is difficult to tell the victims from the actors.

Act Two

EDWARD: Tiresias, there is corruption in the city . . .
FIGURE: There is always corruption in the city . . .
EDWARD *(His voice rising)*: There is *fatal* corruption . . .
FIGURE: I do not need to be spoken to in that tone of voice by a boy wonder.
EDWARD *(Coldly)*: How dare you! The effrontery! I should call for the guards, the soldiers . . .
FIGURE *(Simply sits there.)*: The guards have marched back into their cardboard box, the soldiers have been melted down for lead . . .
EDWARD *(Controlling himself)*: Who is the source of the corruption?
FIGURE: There is something rotten in the palace.
[*Tiny pause.*]
EDWARD: *You're* in the palace.
FIGURE *(Much more coldly)*: But only at your request. Your insistence, you might say. *(Straining his neck around)* Awfully hot, isn't it?
EDWARD *(Sharply)*: I didn't ask you here for small talk.
FIGURE: I let you know I didn't want to come. I sent a messenger saying I didn't want to come. That should have been enough.
EDWARD: I want the truth.
FIGURE: You know it. Your *pretending* not to know it is the only lie.
EDWARD *(With rising anger)*: I warn you . . .
FIGURE *(Sharply)*: Don't warn *me*, Edward. You forget what we were . . .
EDWARD: The blind leading the gauche . . .
FIGURE: I did my best for you, when you came to me at night, trembling, asking me what it is to be a King. "Tiresias, make me a King," you'd cry. I'm a seer, not a magician. You used to *beg* to stay . . .
EDWARD: What was I? Sixteen? Seventeen? You had your little game. "I'm blind," you'd say. "Come closer, boy, and let me touch you." *(Imitating voice of TIRESIAS)*: "Is that

a chest? Is that a leg? Is that a *thigh?*" You touched me here, there, and everywhere . . .

FIGURE: You needed to be loved . . .

EDWARD: Yes. But not by an old man.

FIGURE: How about an old woman?

EDWARD: Be careful, Tiresias. The time for clever foolery is over . . .

FIGURE *(Very sharply)*: What do you want?

EDWARD: The truth about the past.

FIGURE: You're refreshing, at least: everyone else wants to know the truth about the future.

EDWARD *(A command)*: *Tell* me.

FIGURE: Let it go. For both our sakes. And for hers, too.

EDWARD *(With temper now)*: No, I have to know . . . *(HE grabs FIGURE's wrist. FIGURE rises from chair with a surprising nimbleness.)*

FIGURE *(Starting out)*: Goodbye. *(As if someone had sprung up to help him.)* I can manage by myself. *(Ironically)* Thank you. *(Slight pause)* I've enjoyed it—really—*(With great emphasis, slowly, and with contempt)* This great big murder picnic for Greeks.

EDWARD: Stay! [*FIGURE continues slowly out.*] And you're not going to help me? *(Screaming)* You coward! [*FIGURE stops.*]

FIGURE *(His old hold over EDWARD)*: We're in very good voice today, aren't we? *(Then with force and bitterness)* You're past helping. *I'm* the one who needs help . . . I'm blind, feeble . . . I wanted to die in peace . . .

EDWARD: You will. You're the kind who will.

FIGURE: I'm not the only one who needs help. I sit down there surrounded by faces I can't see. But I can sense what they're like. Old battlefields under water. Lighthouses without lights. Eyes that light doesn't change or fire warm. They're ignorant, frightened, ill. They're *your* people. But they don't know what you ARE!

EDWARD *(Beginning of pain now)*: What *am* I? [*FIGURE*

Act Two

has stopped, but HE is silent. The silence hangs.] Don't make me beg you the way I used to. I was arrogant—I was hateful—but I was lonely. *(Bitterly)* I thought you knew . . .

FIGURE: I knew, but I also knew why.

EDWARD: I was afraid to move in any direction, in any direction but away. And then I came less and less to know where "away" was. How far did I have to go to evade . . . *(His voice breaks.)* to evade . . .

FIGURE *(Quietly, but with authority)*: You didn't go quite far enough. *(Pause)* I was born with the future in my head. I foresaw it before it happened.

EDWARD: Then why didn't you stop me, why didn't you tell me, why didn't you save us . . . ?

FIGURE: There are a hundred roads, a thousand fields. Why did you walk down one or cross another? Why didn't you stay put, as wise and as safe as a stone? You didn't have to talk to the Sphinx. You didn't have to marry the Queen. You heard the prophecy. Why didn't you become a fisherman? Or a farmer? Why did you risk *anything*, knowing what you knew?

EDWARD: I was a Prince. I led a charmed life. How could I be *nothing* . . .

FIGURE: Well, you're something *now*. Apollo was your mortar. Delphi was your pestle. And they ground you fine.

EDWARD: I didn't know . . .

FIGURE: Who will ever know what you knew or what you didn't know? It's what you *did* that will make you famous. *(Quickly)* Why don't you ask the question, Edward?

EDWARD: I don't know it . . .

FIGURE: You know it.

EDWARD: I've changed my mind . . .

FIGURE: Then I'll ask it for you. *(Very loudly)*: WHY DID I CHOOSE THIS LIFE?

EDWARD: I never chose it. You know that. I stumbled into the center of the design.

FIGURE: Yes, that's true.

EDWARD: Well? How could I stumble and also choose?

FIGURE: What a fool you are! You *stumbled* into the center . . . but you *chose* the design. Don't you know that?

EDWARD: No, I don't know that.

FIGURE: All right. I'll change the question. *(Very loudly)*: WHY DID THE GODS CHOOSE ME?

EDWARD: Yes, why? Answer that!

FIGURE: All Kings are cursed, all men are cursed.

EDWARD: *Answer* it.

FIGURE: You don't see the *grand* design, Edward. Why is the runner crippled and the cobbler's right hand warped? And the painter's eye put out and the musician's ear turned deaf? Why does the innocent child run under the chariot wheel? Who orders the water to drown the strongest swimmer? The finest mind to go slack and the keenest wit to go dumb? A foot may be ripped of its flesh . . .

EDWARD *(Yells)*: NO!

FIGURE: The bone crushed by steel . . .

EDWARD: NO!

FIGURE: Two feet be tightly bound . . .

EDWARD: Stop . . . please . . .

FIGURE: Don't blame anyone, Edward. Blame the gods.

EDWARD *(With great bitterness)*: I . . . blame . . . you . . . all. [*Pause*]

FIGURE: WHY AM I BLIND, EDWARD? WHO . . . MADE . . . ME . . . BLIND?

EDWARD *(HE understands the implication of the question HE never thought to ask, but HE doesn't know how to deal with it.)* I didn't ask you here . . .

FIGURE: No. You forced me here. *(Pause)* You love yourself, Edward, but it's not an affair of the heart. Even that's a play . . . of keys, doors, mirrors . . . of settings and costumes . . .

EDWARD: Is that all you have to tell me?

FIGURE: That's all.

EDWARD *(This is his question.)*: WILL . . . WE . . . LIVE?

Act Two

FIGURE *(Ambiguously)*: You will live . . . on.

EDWARD *(Dismissing FIGURE)*: You and I will not see each other again.

FIGURE *(With bitter laugh)*: I've *never* seen you. *(Pause)* I wouldn't be so cavalier about the sensuality of the blind, if I were you. It's a way of knowing the world . . .

EDWARD: Goodbye . . .

FIGURE *(On way out)*: You always had very fine skin, Edward. Be careful you don't get burned.

[*EDWARD stands in a fixed position. FIGURE collides with or is intercepted by the QUEEN as SHE enters and HE attempts to leave right stage.*]

FIGURE: Hello. [*No response*] Hello. [*No response*] . . . Your Majesty.

QUEEN *(Turning)*: And who are you *now*?

FIGURE: Myself . . . as I have always been. *(HE puts down cane, takes off dark glasses.)*

QUEEN: But you're so fickle . . .

FIGURE: Not really. Behind the flashing lights, the battery stays steady. *(Indicating EDWARD)* Do you want him here?

QUEEN: No.

FIGURE: There's a way of getting him off. I can make him disappear as fast as you can say "Greek tragedy."

QUEEN *(Hesitating)*: It won't kill him, will it?

FIGURE: Not really.

QUEEN: "Greek tragedy." [*EDWARD exits.*] There's something I'd like to talk to you about. Seriously, I mean. If we survive, I . . .

FIGURE *(Humorously)*: Do you think you have a chance?

QUEEN: If not as ourselves, then as more than ourselves—stereotypes, archetypes . . .

FIGURE: *Type* types.

QUEEN: You see, just because I'm mature doesn't mean that I *feel* mature.

FIGURE: Oh?

QUEEN: I don't know if you'll understand . . .

The Palace at 4 A.M.

FIGURE: Go ahead. Try me.
QUEEN: You won't laugh?
FIGURE: I promise.
QUEEN: Do you think I'm old enough . . . to live alone?
FIGURE *(Starts to laugh, begins to get out of control.)*: You? Oh, yes! *(Howls)* Old enough? *You?* *(HE breaks into laughter once again.)*
QUEEN: It's not *that* funny. It's not that funny at all.
FIGURE: Oh, it is, it is. *(Through tears)* Are the Pyramids old enough? Is the Nile? *(Again laughing)*
QUEEN: I'll just wait here till you stop.
FIGURE *(Controlling himself)*: I'm sorry. By the way . . . *are* you thinking of living alone?
QUEEN: It's crossed my mind. The quiet. The privacy. The lack of constant surveillance.
FIGURE: The *lone*liness.
QUEEN: There's that, of course. But sometimes loneliness can be . . . creative. Fruitful.
FIGURE: About surveillance: It's *your* little eyes pressed tight to the keyhole, *your* little pen scratching away at the record, adding, revising, figuring it all out . . .
QUEEN *(Really irritated)*: The question I asked is: Am I old *enough* to live alone?
FIGURE *(Airily, to let her know he can play her game)*: Don't you think that's sort of been settled? Unless you'd like to add something. Wrinkles? Liver spots? Years, perhaps? *(Suddenly and very cruelly)* You used to be very good in bed, I hear.
QUEEN *(SHE lets the words stay in the air and fade.)*: In Venice, the gondolas are shifting in the canals. In Nice, the sunset is settling down . . . *(SHE closes her eyes.)* I'd give all Thebes for a little peace and quiet.
FIGURE: Would you like to see a pageant depicting the words "A little peace and quiet" performed by the children of Thebes?
QUEEN: And what would the children of Thebes be doing

Act Two

up at this hour?

FIGURE: Too young to be alone—as some of us are too old—they must stay with their parents. And since their parents are waiting and waiting for some resolution to the events of the day . . .

QUEEN: . . . night . . .

FIGURE: . . . night, why, the children are up. With their parents.

QUEEN: That is a satisfactory explanation. I would not, however, like to see a pageant. Thank you. Thank you very much.

FIGURE *(Breezily, waving a hand in the air)*: It's nothing.

QUEEN *(Getting back to serious business)*: About my question: *Should* I live alone? You seem rather evasive.

FIGURE: It seems to me a wise decision. Since we die alone, why not live alone?

QUEEN: I could think of arguments on the other side.

FIGURE: You *have*. One of your big arguments just left.

QUEEN *(Looks at him, almost decides to let this go, but not quite.)*: You've never been married, have you?

FIGURE: No. Being a Fool, I decided not to gild the lily. The word "relationship" always sends a slight shiver down my back. When people talk about their "relationships," I feel as if I were listening to a dog trying to sing. I feel . . . sorry.

QUEEN *(Ironically)*: How much sympathy we have . . . for the people we don't know!

FIGURE: In any case, I think you *should* live alone. It is always better to be prepared for the inevitable.

QUEEN: If something's inevitable, what difference if you're prepared or not? It's for what's unpredictable that one should be prepared. You can't spend your whole life just getting ready to die.

FIGURE: Oh, but millions do!

QUEEN: I've been getting ready. But I do little things on the side. *(Icily)* Like ruling a country.

FIGURE: You're not ruling it very well. If you were, we

wouldn't be stranded here, two sharks, and one pilot fish, with the level of the water in the tank going down.

QUEEN *(Suddenly frightened)*: Water? It's air I worry about.

FIGURE: As well you should. *(Too hastily)* As well we *all* should.

QUEEN: Do you feel there's something in the air—as if it were too wet, burdened with something—as if it thickened slightly each time it went in and out of your lungs?

FIGURE: Well . . . *(HE hesitates.)* It *is* a heavy night . . . there have been storms and stillnesses, oddities in the sky.

QUEEN *(The girlish side, the lady in distress)*: You know, I need a friend desperately . . . Someone to be . . . *(For the first time, SHE doesn't know what SHE wants to say.)*

FIGURE: To be light?

QUEEN: No, not light. Someone who would say, "But my dear, of course it will all turn out right in the end." Someone who could convince me of that.

FIGURE: And you think such a person would be a friend?

QUEEN *(Unsure but defiant)*: Yes.

FIGURE: You would have a liar for a friend, Your Majesty.

QUEEN *(Sadly)*: How odd that sounded suddenly! Your Majesty!

FIGURE: Without the trappings of power, Your Majesty, the powerful are remarkably like everyone else.

QUEEN: I don't think that. Human, yes. Who can escape it? Except animals. And monsters.

FIGURE: And angels.

QUEEN: But people can be powerful in themselves. I don't mean physical strength, of course . . .

FIGURE: It's a *form* of power.

QUEEN: A very primitive form. Then we might as well have bears for kings, and elephants for queens, and give everything over to size and muscle.

FIGURE: And what would you say power really is?

QUEEN: Knowing you're going to die and knowing who

you are. And then, to be brutally frank, not letting anyone get too close. You should know yourself, but not let yourself be known.

FIGURE: Ah, but if you know you're going to die, you need to be comforted. It's such a temptation to share yourself with someone, to give a piece of yourself away.

QUEEN: And how does one do that? By rending flesh? By tearing off little inches of cells and hair and skin and handing them over? No, no, no.

FIGURE: There's the heart. Unless I'm talking to someone heartless? Could I possibly be doing that?

QUEEN: You'll have to judge for yourself. *(SHE looks at him coldly, turns her back on him, and sits down on the bench very quietly. The effect SHE desires to convey is: he no longer exists. To herself, starting out lightly, but immediately overcome by emotion.)* Somewhere there must be dancing and lights and people who aren't waiting . . . *(SHE bursts into tears.)* I feel so sorry for them. I feel sorry for myself. I don't want them to die. I don't want to die. I never, never wanted all this . . .

FIGURE *(Now very cruelly, moving in for the kill)*: Admit it. *(Very loud voice, very emphasized)* YOU KNEW WHO HE WAS ALL THE TIME!

QUEEN *(Horrified, gets up.)*: No. No. I did not.

FIGURE: I say you did. Oh, maybe it wasn't right in the front of your mind, maybe it was one tiny fraction behind, but it was somewhere very close . . . you could smell your own blood, you could taste your own skin . . . You were making love to yourself!

QUEEN: That would be a more apt description of *him!*

FIGURE: No. You.

QUEEN: You liar! Liar! Fake!

FIGURE: You would do anything for love . . . or what you call love. Because it's power. Everything is subsumed under one heading. And the boy hero, the great unriddler of the Sphinx . . . who else was fit for the Queen? Who else would

be so passionate in bed, so wanting to be King? Who else would rouse the cheers of the populace, ever ready to shout "Hero!" "Savior!" "Leader!"
  QUEEN *(Calling for help)*: Edward!
  FIGURE: Truth, truth, truth, truth.
  QUEEN *(Calling, commanding)*: Edward! Don't let him, Edward!
  FIGURE: Face it. You did what all leaders do. They move toward self-satisfaction and power. You're no different.
  QUEEN: I didn't know you stored up so much hatred. Why do you hate me so?
  FIGURE *(Very slowly)*: Because . . . I . . . once . . . felt . . . lust . . . for . . . a . . . Queen. Because my birth, and only my birth, keeps me from standing where he stood, from lying where he lay, from . . .
  QUEEN *(Beginning to gain control again, interrupting him)*: . . . from a fate I don't think people like you are prepared to meet.
  FIGURE: Why not? Since I'm going to die, I'd just as soon die famous.
  QUEEN *(With contempt)*: But you're famous already, my dear. Simply by standing ten yards away from me, your immortality is assured. And now you know that, please go.
  FIGURE *(Half wanting to know, half cunningly)*: You never found me . . . appealing?
  QUEEN *(Coldly)*: No.
  FIGURE: Not in any way? Not even my . . . *charm?*
  QUEEN: Oh, my poor dear . . .
  FIGURE: My hands . . . say? One finger?
  QUEEN: I've never noticed your hands, or your fingers . . .
  FIGURE *(Suddenly and terrifyingly, HE takes her neck in his hands as if to choke her.)*: Do you notice them now? *(HE lets go.)* [*Strangling sounds from her*] *(With great venom, at last)* You silly bitch. You stupid Queen. *(HE exits.)*
  [*Stage darkens. SHE stands there quietly, expressing no emotion, as the light fades around her. There is a distant*

Act Two

rumble of thunder. Then another, closer. Slowly, from either side of the stage, two mirrors glide onto the stage. They must be full-length, tall enough to hide a human body, and reach down to the stage floor. They may be wheeled in, carried in, rolled on—any device that works. They need not literally be mirrors as long as they clearly represent mirrors to the audience. The desired effect is one of two long mirrors moving onto the stage of their own volition. The mirrors stop, to the right and left of stage center. One mirror moves in front of the QUEEN *and obliterates her image completely.* EDWARD *steps out from behind the other mirror. The stage is in half light.*]

EDWARD: I've stood on a battlement and withdrawn from the edge, afraid not of falling but that I might suddenly hurl myself down! I have opened a closet door and been transfixed by the sense of someone on the other side opening it for me—someone invisible but present. When my hand reaches down toward a glass case, another hand rises up to meet it. When I turn the corner of the street, the shadow that I cast is beginning to have an indelible outline. In my mirror, a man who resembles me is walking forward to greet me. His eyelids are gradually being carved, his arms sculptured. Soon he will be marble from head to foot.

QUEEN *(Steps out from behind other mirror and seats herself beside* EDWARD. *Puts her head on his shoulder)*: How fast the time goes . . . and how slow! [HE *puts his arms around her.*] I looked out of my bedroom window down into the square. They were still there, massed and silent. Torches lit up their faces; women carrying sick babies; spindle-legged children, their arms covered with sores; emaciated men, shivering with fever. They are in a huge circle—huddled, cold, miserable.

[*A clock strikes four times.*]

EDWARD: It is 4 A.M.—too far away from last night, and not close enough to tomorrow morning. It is the dead center of nothing. I think we are about to begin . . . the beginning of the end.

[*THEY rise and come forward.*]

QUEEN *(Pauses, shyly)*: You know, I'm afraid to look at myself in the mirror. Even if *I* don't get older, the mirror must.

EDWARD: Don't be silly. It renews itself on our decay. It reflects what it wants us to see.

QUEEN: *Have* to see. Well—I'll look in yours but I won't look in mine.

EDWARD: Don't you trust yours? Mine tells the truth.

QUEEN: As *you* see it.

EDWARD: I'll look. *(HE looks into his mirror.)*

QUEEN: What do you see?

EDWARD: Only myself.

QUEEN: As you desire to be?

EDWARD: I desire to be as I am. I see a King, young . . .

QUEEN: You've given me courage. *(SHE looks into hers.)*

EDWARD: And you? What do you see?

QUEEN: A woman of a certain style . . . and age. Not bad, really. A month in Switzerland in the hands of the right butcher . . .

EDWARD: Let me see. *(HE walks over and looks at her reflection in mirror.)*

QUEEN: What do you think?

EDWARD *(Staggers back, his voice rising)*: I . . . I see . . .

QUEEN *(Turning)*: What is it?

EDWARD *(Recovering himself)*: Nothing. Nothing.

QUEEN: No. What did you see?

EDWARD: You . . .

QUEEN: But you're shaking! What's the matter?

EDWARD: I was surprised, that's all . . . by the . . . accuracy of the reflection.

QUEEN: A famous quality of mirrors. Let me look in yours. Stand in front of it. *(HE does. SHE looks. Pained, frightened.)* Oh! Oh!

Act Two

EDWARD: Don't tell me. No! *Tell me!*
QUEEN: Nothing. A blind light . . .
EDWARD: Blind?
QUEEN: No . . . blinding . . . I meant to say "blinding" . . . And in mine you saw . . . ?
EDWARD: I *told* you. Nothing.
QUEEN *(Slowly)*: You're lying. Worse than that, you're avoiding something.
EDWARD *(With false bravado, uneasily)*: You're a mind reader, a clairvoyant . . .
QUEEN: What is it?
EDWARD *(The unpleasant liar pointlessly trying to gain time)*: How many times do I have to tell you?
QUEEN: You've told me so many things . . .
EDWARD: I made a mistake. *(HE won't really admit it.)* Maybe.
QUEEN: When?
EDWARD: Some time before 4 A.M.
QUEEN: You *didn't*.
EDWARD: I went down.
QUEEN *(With very sharp edge to her voice)*: And?
EDWARD: I talked to the blind man.
QUEEN: You asked the question.
EDWARD: I asked the question.
QUEEN: And did he answer it?
EDWARD: Yes.
QUEEN: Let me sit down . . . [*HE leads her to throne.*] *(SHE stares into space.)* Well, that's that, then.
EDWARD: We never had a chance, and you know it.
QUEEN: We had a tiny chance, the smallest mouse of a chance. It's strange; I'm thinking of far-off places. Finland, Greenland . . .
EDWARD: Any place but here?
QUEEN: Any time but now . . . *(Not directed to him or audience but to space, a memory.)* When I was a young girl, how I loved position! The bowing and scraping, the dancing

feet that stopped or started at my command. The deference! I wanted to manipulate and control. I would lean forward—and the contours of a city would change. I would lean back—and a state would disappear. In my sleep, I redrew the lines of a hundred maps. But one day, I looked at myself naked... I saw what I was... I bled when the moon turned, like any common woman; I was prey to the same infections as the court. The idea of power slipped away... I was left alone to struggle with its shadow...

EDWARD *(Another set piece)*: And I have been stiff and aloof. I watched my fate like a man on top of a mountain examining an ant, miles away, through binoculars. Suddenly, I was down at the foot of the mountain, grappling. I became the very ant I assumed I was watching.

QUEEN: The great mistake is knowing one's fate in advance. *(Slight pause)* To end up in a little jewel box filled with bones!

[*Shouts from window: "Kill, kill, kill, kill."*]

EDWARD *(Wryly)*: They've changed the lyrics. *(Listening hard, like a doomed man hoping for hope.)* Or is it "King, King, King"?

QUEEN *(Looking at him hard. Slowly)*: No, I don't think so.

[*EDWARD walks over to his mirror, the QUEEN to hers. The following, very stylized, is addressed by each of them to a mirror rather than to each other.*]

EDWARD: Well, here we are.

QUEEN: Again.

EDWARD: And again and again and again.

QUEEN: If we could make time stop!

EDWARD *(Each syllable of "practically" prolonged)*: We practically have.

QUEEN: I heard the first bird.

EDWARD: Chirp. Tweet. Chirp.

QUEEN: We meet for the last time.

EDWARD: The last time *this* time.

Act Two

QUEEN: Edward, when you asked me out . . .
EDWARD: My dear, when you asked me *in* . . .
QUEEN: The dark is all the same.
EDWARD: It comes around in time.
QUEEN: What are you going to do?
EDWARD: Wait and wait. And you?
QUEEN: No. I think I'll think.
EDWARD: Think about what? You?
QUEEN *(Turns around and sits down.)*: I heard the second bird.
EDWARD *(Wheels around abruptly and walks over to her.)*: Stop it!
QUEEN *(Innocently)*: Stop what?
EDWARD: This dialogue. I'm not interested in birds . . .
QUEEN: This is so typical of you.
EDWARD: Really?
QUEEN: Yes. It was not only *my* dialogue, you know. I thought I heard a voice chirping back . . .
EDWARD: You're bird-crazy this morning.
QUEEN: What a suburban thing to say! We might be sitting at breakfast, about to have another cup of coffee . . .
EDWARD *(Maliciously)*: Would you like another cup of coffee? The flies are delicious here.
QUEEN *(Starts on the word "flies.")*: Now *you* stop it.
EDWARD *(Innocently)*: Stop what?
QUEEN: *You* know.
EDWARD: Yes. I know the whole miserable story now. No matter what, you're older. The responsibility rests on you.
QUEEN: The whole story? It might just be a tissue of lies from the beginning.
EDWARD: Your neck and my eyes.
QUEEN: One neck . . . one pair of eyes . . .
EDWARD: But *ours*, my dear. That makes such a difference. They're dying like . . . flies . . .
QUEEN: What a gift for a phrase!
EDWARD: . . . flies down there. And do you seriously

care? Do you really give a damn? You can read the casualty reports, you can look at the accident statistics . . . They're oh, so far away . . .

QUEEN: What happens down there happens. We're still safe in this room.

EDWARD: As if you believe it!

QUEEN: I believe it from moment to moment. I believe it as long as I breathe. I know the play so well I can enjoy the intermission.

EDWARD: The hot breath of the intermission becomes the little dragon of . . . *(Gives her an obsequious bow as if waiting for her to conclude the line.)*

QUEEN: The end?

EDWARD: You read my thoughts and I'll read yours.

QUEEN: I'm trying not to be afraid.

EDWARD: I know what you're afraid of. I said you were *old*.

QUEEN: I don't think age matters when you have fifteen minutes . . .

EDWARD: Oh, doesn't it? Fifteen minutes or forever, some of us are older and some of us are younger.

QUEEN: A statement that could hardly be disputed.

EDWARD: Then stop disputing it, stop playing games. *(With rising anger)* I didn't ask for this, I didn't ask to be born!

QUEEN: Nor did I. Did that ever occur to you? I was the child of a King and a Queen. Like you. I know more about your feelings than anyone. But about mine! You know nothing.

EDWARD: You created me, you allowed me to be abandoned . . .

QUEEN: Allowed! Everything in my life has been allowed. I did very little of the allowing. *You* should be familiar with power. The powerful are held in their own grip.

EDWARD: The natural fight, they fight for what's theirs. Did you? You should have recognized me by my skin, my smell. A cat, a spider, an ant does better. They wound, they kill . . . but they do not wound their own!

QUEEN: Battles are lost by someone. You're looking at a loser. You don't think I suffered?

EDWARD *(Hesitating, then)*: No.

QUEEN: Then you know nothing about me. For ten years I walked around empty, heartsick . . . I was a formal mask, a convention . . . I was nothing . . . flesh under cloth . . . a mere consideration of cloth . . .

EDWARD: Don't ask me to pity you.

QUEEN: I don't.

EDWARD: You made me a monster!

QUEEN: Your inability to see me, to love me—*that* is what is monstrous . . . I'll tell you the true meaning of horror: to lie in bed with another and feel inexpressibly alone. The howling wastes of the Arctic are nothing to the millimeter of space that separates one lover from another.

EDWARD: There's so much talk about love, and so little of it.

QUEEN: Because of people like you.

EDWARD: No. Because people like you have made people like me what I am.

QUEEN: *You* made *me* up. I'm nothing but thirteen hundred bones at your disposal. You wanted a story—well, stories must have endings. You wanted power—well, power gets struck down. You wanted me—but as part of the story, part of the power. They all come together.

EDWARD: I don't believe you ever loved me.

QUEEN: Oh, Edward, but I did!

EDWARD: Is it getting darker?

QUEEN: It is always getting darker, Edward. That's the price of growing older. The sun rises but you're already aware of night. And then time goes so much faster.

EDWARD: Will you be sad to leave me?

QUEEN: Oh, yes.

EDWARD: And . . . anyone else?

QUEEN: I'll be sad to leave myself.

EDWARD *(Looks at her carefully.)* Sadder than to leave me?

QUEEN *(Sparing him, but trying not to lie)*: I don't know, Edward.

EDWARD *(Not convincingly)*: I'll be sad, too.

QUEEN: I hope so . . . and I hope not. *(Suddenly rising)*: Edward, the story is over.

EDWARD: Very nearly, I guess.

QUEEN *(Very sweetly now)*: Edward, if I *was* guilty, *am* guilty, forgive me.

EDWARD: And you, too. Forgive me.

QUEEN: Of course. You were sweet to ask me out . . .

EDWARD: Is that what I did?

QUEEN: I think so.

EDWARD: Well, it went very fast . . .

QUEEN: Yes, it seems to have. We had a love affair . . .

EDWARD: And a murder.

QUEEN: I wonder if there's really any difference.

EDWARD: There's supposed to be.

QUEEN: Oh, *suppose* . . .

EDWARD: People do things to one another . . .

QUEEN: *That* they do.

EDWARD: They don't have much choice. *We* didn't.

QUEEN: Not power so much, not even love . . . just not to be alone.

EDWARD: Yes.

QUEEN: Do you know what loneliness is, Edward?

EDWARD: I think I do.

QUEEN: It's Narcissus not seeing himself in the pool. *(Slight pause)* I must go, Edward.

EDWARD *(Now more childishly, more babyishly)*: Don't leave me yet.

QUEEN: I have to. You know that . . .

EDWARD: I'm afraid of dying.

QUEEN: So am I.

Act Two

EDWARD: Tell me I won't yet.
QUEEN: You won't . . . yet.
EDWARD: But . . . when?
QUEEN: I don't know that. Goodbye.
EDWARD: Stay! A second! [SHE starts off.] (Loudly) I don't want to see it!
QUEEN (Turning): What you did to me, or what I did to you?
EDWARD: I don't want to see it!
QUEEN: There's only one way not to see it, Edward.
EDWARD: Don't say it!
QUEEN: You know the way.
EDWARD: Just a little longer—a piece of a second, and then a piece of that.
QUEEN: Do you think I will . . . feel pain?
EDWARD (Shutting his eyes): I don't want to feel it!
QUEEN: Oh, Edward, how can I spare you *my* fate?
EDWARD: Don't walk out of the room!
QUEEN: It's no longer a room—it is becoming an occasion, an ending.
EDWARD: Don't go through the door!
QUEEN: I must, Edward.
EDWARD: Please!
QUEEN (Starts to exit, very simply.): I loved you.
EDWARD: Love me *now!* Love me again!
QUEEN: I do. I do. (As SHE is about to exit, says with pity): Edward, I'd stay . . . if I could. But I am not even myself anymore.
EDWARD: Don't leave me! [SHE exits.] (Calling after her): Don't leave me!

[*The stage goes dark. An absolutely blood-curdling scream. As SHE screams, the QUEEN'S mirror is lit. In it, the image of a hanged woman—by projection, using the shadow of a dummy, or by any theatrical device that works. Then, FIGURE enters, as light comes up, but not all the way, on EDWARD. FIGURE hands EDWARD a mask on a stick, but* hands it to him backwards so that audience can't see its image. EDWARD takes it, turns it around. It is the mask of a blind man, the eyes bloodied, the blood running down the mask. At the same time, FIGURE hands EDWARD a blind-man's cane.]

EDWARD *(From behind mask)*: My eyes! My eyes! My eyes! *(EDWARD comes forward toward footlights. As HE does, FIGURE exits at same pace toward left. EDWARD, using the blind-man's cane, gropes his way across the stage toward the footlights, and reaches the stage apron. But, miscalculating, the stick probes empty air in front of the stage apron. Shocked, HE drops his cane into the orchestra pit and steps back. To audience, imploring slowly, with equal emphasis on both words)*: HELP . . . ME.

CURTAIN

THE FOLDING GREEN

A Play in Three Acts

For Jean Stafford

THE FOLDING GREEN was first performed by the Poet's Theatre, Cambridge, Mass., on 24 November, 1958, with the following cast:

Elena	DEE FRENCH
Ramona	MARTHA DOW
John	LYLE J. LORENTZ
A Hooded Figure	LYLE J. LORENTZ
An Old Woman	CHARLOTTE TEJESSY
Dr. Warren Lathrop	DONALD CERULLI
Donald Ashberry	CARMACK OAKLEY
Cora Ashberry	MAURA K. WEDGE
Teresa Jones	HJORDIS HUNE
Felicity	JUDY O'KEEFFE
Gilbert de Cordovan	JON ADAMS
Baron Rothschild	LYLE J. LORENTZ
The Guardian at the Gate	TOM BENTLEY

Director, Otto Ashermann
Design and sets, Allen Klein
Costumes, Catharine Huntington and Sydney Osborne
Lights, Pema

THE FOLDING GREEN was first performed in New York by the Playwrights Unit, Theatre Vandam, on 2 November, 1964, with the following cast:

Elena	NANCY CUSHMAN
Ramona	HELEN NOYES
John	CLINTON ANDERSON
A Figure	CLINTON ANDERSON
A Woman	ALICE BEARDSLEY
Dr. Lawrence Hawley	JOEL THOMAS
Donald Ashberry	ROBERT KIRK
Cora Ashberry	JANET SARNO
Teresa Jones	JANET DOWD
Felicity	GWYDA DON-HOWE

Director, Warren Enters
Design and sets, Thomas Wentland
Costumes, Cynthia Pennell
Lights, Walter Cavalieri

ACT ONE

Elena's living room. A winter morning.

ACT TWO

SCENE ONE: The attic. A few days later.

SCENE TWO: The living room. Immediately following.

ACT THREE

The living room, Three months later.

CHARACTERS

ELENA DE CORDOVAN BARBRIDGE, *a rich old woman*
RAMONA, *her companion*
FELICITY, *her ward*
CORA ASHBERRY, *her daughter*
DONALD ASHBERRY, *her son-in-law*
DR. LAWRENCE HAWLEY
TERESA JONES, *her friend*
JOHN, *her butler**
A FIGURE, *wearing a hood**
A WOMAN, *wearing a cape*

*Played by the same actor.

ACT ONE

SCENE: *ELENA's living room. Expensively but not necessarily realistically furnished. The time is now. A winter morning.*

AT RISE: *ELENA and RAMONA are facing each other across a table. There is a crystal ball between them. A cane leans against ELENA's chair. They are sipping champagne. A champagne bucket with a bottle in it is at RAMONA's feet.*

ELENA: Put some money in the plate.
RAMONA: There's ten thousand dollars in the kitty already and not a peep out of them. More champagne?
ELENA: A sip. I can't understand why no one's materializing. Last week the kitty was a mere three hundred and we got Charlotte Brontë.
RAMONA: We asked for Tolstoy.
ELENA: This damn snow! They can't get through.
RAMONA: Whom are we trying for?
ELENA: Baron Rothschild.
RAMONA: Why?
ELENA: I want to ask him something.
RAMONA: What?
ELENA: Whether to convert some debentures. You wouldn't understand. Keep your hands flat.
RAMONA: They *are* flat. Almost as flat as this champagne.
ELENA: John! [*JOHN, the butler, enters.*]
JOHN: Madame?
ELENA: The bubbles have disappeared.
JOHN: Yes, madame. [*JOHN exits.*]
RAMONA: He's looking more tacky every day. His butler's outfit's developing a patina.

ELENA: I wouldn't mention clothes if I were you. I bought you a wardrobe twenty years ago and you've yet to wear the second dress!

RAMONA: My fluffy evening gown with the green folds? I've been saving it. I thought when I came here I'd meet a young man . . .

ELENA: Why don't you face it? You've gotten too old to tell one young man from another.

RAMONA: I haven't. I met a young person on the street yesterday. I think he took a shine to me. He . . .

ELENA: You've been thinking that sort of thing for years. Last time the man came to fix the furnace, you were beside yourself with whimsy. You practically threw yourself into the dustbin.

RAMONA: I'd be married now if Freddie's Great Dane hadn't turned on him.

ELENA: Two whole decades in red! Don't you get sick of it?

RAMONA: Freddie thought it was becoming.

ELENA: Maybe it was *then*.

RAMONA: Freddie said I was that rare woman who could wear anything. He said . . .

ELENA: I'm bored.

RAMONA: You always get bored when we talk about me, but never when we talk about *you*.

ELENA: I know a fascinating subject when I hear one.

[*JOHN brings in champagne, removes old bottle, places new one in bucket.*]

JOHN: More Mumm. [*HE exits.*]

RAMONA *(Yawning)*: Why don't we try for a queen?

ELENA: And get Elizabeth down again with all that advice about the Armada?

RAMONA: Well, what do you expect from a dead virgin?

ELENA: If I were a virgin, at least I'd be well-read. And I say if you're a dead queen, live up to it.

RAMONA: How can a dead queen live? . . .

Act One

ELENA: God! Communicating with you is like shouting through rice pudding. Can't you make yourself more intelligent?
RAMONA: Freddie found me sufficiently lively. And don't forget: when you're a hundred, I'll only be ninety-five.
ELENA: And you'll probably still be wearing that dress.
RAMONA: Hostility. I never respond to hostility.
ELENA: It's too late to be mawkish. Is the table tipping?
RAMONA: Not yet. Shall I pour?
ELENA: Keep one hand flat while you do it.
RAMONA: You are going to leave me a lot of money, aren't you?
ELENA: What is money, after all? National heroes printed on green to evoke envy.
RAMONA: People who have lots of it are always making little philosophical remarks about it. I don't care what it is; I care what it does. You can't buy champagne without money.
ELENA: You don't have a cent and you're drinking it like a fish.
RAMONA: Well, I'm your companion. I try to share your experiences. At least I don't flatter you like some of your so-called friends.
ELENA: Who, for instance?
RAMONA: Dr. Lathrop, for one. The way he pampers your imaginary illnesses!
ELENA: You imagine they're imaginary. My life is a battlefield and my internal organs are in the front line. When they fail, whose companion will you be?
RAMONA: There are other rich old ladies in New York.
ELENA: None rich enough to keep *you* in champagne.
RAMONA: I felt something!
ELENA: Hold on! [*The lights dim, the table rocks, there is a flash of smoke. When the smoke clears, a FIGURE, wearing a hood, is standing by the table.*] Baron Rothschild?
FIGURE: Is this the Newark Airport?
ELENA: No. This is the private residence of Elena de Cor-

63

The Folding Green

dovan Barbridge in New York City. Who are you?
FIGURE: That's what I came to find out.
RAMONA: You mean you're not a celebrated figure?
FIGURE: Of course I am. I just don't know which one.
ELENA: A dud! Don't you have *any* idea who you are?
FIGURE *(To RAMONA)*: Who are you?
RAMONA: My name is Ramona. I'm her companion.
FIGURE: An exacting occupation, I imagine. [*The table shakes, smoke, etc.*]
ELENA: There it goes again! Come in, come in, whoever you are!
[*A small, gnarled WOMAN, wearing a cape, appears.*]
WOMAN: Lordie me! What weather! This is a pleasant place to rest after the journey.
ELENA: Journey from where?
WOMAN: From a place I am no longer at.
RAMONA: Do you know anything about the folding green?
WOMAN: What language are you speaking?
RAMONA: Clams. Mazoola.
ELENA: Do you know anything about money?
WOMAN: It's what people exchange, between emotions.
ELENA: That's what it *should* be. It has become an emotion in itself.
WOMAN: About love, I know everything.
ELENA: Like what?
WOMAN: Love affairs never end; they merely stop beginning.
ELENA: More facile than profound.
RAMONA: Besides, she's not interested in love any more. She's past the peak.
WOMAN: Nonsense. I'm ninety-eight, and I'm still pursued everywhere.
ELENA: By what?
WOMAN: Tax collectors and the police. What else is there to be pursued by?

Act One

RAMONA *(Giving WOMAN and FIGURE a significant look)*: And do you ever see the Baron Rothschild?

WOMAN: Ah, the Baron Rothschild! Charming man, though a bit of a banker . . .

FIGURE: If you leave Ramona the Russian Imperial . . .

WOMAN *(Poking him in ribs)*: Ha, ha. It's a little poem he learned as a child: "If you leave Ramona the Russian Imperial, / In a kimono, bedraggled, weary, ill . . . "

ELENA: It's on the obscure side. Who's the author?

WOMAN: Anne Ominous. And now, poor dear, he must hurry off. Mustn't you, *son?*

FIGURE *(To WOMAN)*: Will I see you, mother, at the airport?

RAMONA: How nice! They're related!

FIGURE: Soup is thicker than water.

WOMAN: And flight is faster than sound. *(To ELENA)* He gets *so* disoriented. [*FIGURE strides offstage rapidly.*] He's my first and my favorite; the others were bottle-fed. He follows me everywhere.

ELENA: What atrocious taste!

WOMAN *(Going into her routine)*: The message! The message is coming through! Mishmash, Oshkosh, dirty wash. Those who are flesh become spirit; those who become spirit *know*. Remember that, Mrs. Barbridge, when you count your money.

ELENA: It is impossible to count my money. I'm an interlocking directorate who's thrown away the key.

WOMAN: Find out who the others are.

ELENA: What others?

WOMAN: I cannot say more. My flight leaves in a moment.

ELENA: You'll never make it in time in all this snow. Would you like to borrow my chauffeur?

WOMAN: Nothing is so depressing as a borrowed chauffeur. Goodbye, my dears. [*Starts to exit, then turns and looks back at ELENA and RAMONA.*] I just saw you the way you must have looked as little girls.

The Folding Green

ELENA: And how was that?
WOMAN: Ghastly. [*WOMAN exits.*]
ELENA *(Getting up from table)*: Our friends from the other world were odd and useless. I'm going up to get undressed. I have an appointment with Warren, and Teresa's coming to work on the portrait.
RAMONA: I think I'll stay down here and finish my novel.
ELENA: What's it about?
RAMONA: Rich people having a good time while they travel.
ELENA: An impossible theme—they never do. [*SHE picks up cane, starts to leave.*] Don't forget to put the crystal ball at the bottom of the laundry hamper. We need all the vibrations we can get.
RAMONA: I won't.
[*ELENA exits. RAMONA waits till she is out of earshot. Then:*] All right. You can come out now. [*FIGURE and WOMAN appear.*] *(Doling out cash)* Here.
WOMAN: I had to have a voice lesson, madame. And my son had to rent a hood.
RAMONA: Don't itemize the bill. How much do you want?
WOMAN: Fifty, apiece.
RAMONA *(Handing them money)*: Here you are. Next time I'd like a little more conviction. *(To FIGURE)* What a hash you made of the key line!
FIGURE *(Pointing to WOMAN)*: She was late picking me up at the hotel. I wasn't even sure who I was supposed to be.
WOMAN: Shut up!
RAMONA: *I* give the orders.
WOMAN *(To FIGURE)*: What do you think Mrs. Barbridge is—a fool?
FIGURE: I *tried* to get to it again, you know, after I said how soup was thicker . . .
RAMONA *(To WOMAN)*: And you! Why all that nonsense about love? She asked about money, didn't she?

Act One

WOMAN: She used to be interested in love, and I thought if I got to the line right away, it would sound too obvious. Besides, Mrs. Barbridge didn't seem quite herself this morning.

RAMONA: None of your lip. Mrs. Barbridge is a very great woman in a small way. Be silent and take orders. I could lift the phone and get a hundred actresses.

WOMAN: I am not just *any* character actress, madame. I have a letter from Chekhov, a check from Lermontov . . .

RAMONA: Never mind all that. You are not the only character actress thrown out of work because there are no characters any more. I may need you in the next few days. I think she's plotting something. Stay in until you hear from me.

FIGURE: May I make a suggestion, madame?

RAMONA *(Resigned)*: Go ahead.

FIGURE: I think the table should shake a little more.

RAMONA: If the smoke were thicker that wouldn't be necessary. Next time, make the smoke thicker. Good day.

WOMAN and FIGURE: Goodbye, madame. [*THEY exit.*]

RAMONA *(Contemptuously)*: Actors! [*RAMONA exits left as JOHN enters right.*]

JOHN *(To empty room)*: The doctor.

[*As JOHN exits, ELENA, holding her cane in her hand, races across the room, and lies down on a chaise longue. A young man enters in a dark gray suit. Handsome, stiff, cold, correct.*]

LAWRENCE: How do you do, Mrs. Barbridge?

ELENA *(Sitting up)*: But you are not Warren . . . you are not my doctor!

LAWRENCE: Don't be alarmed. Dr. Lathrop is on an emergency in Hawaii. One of his patient's volcanoes erupted. I am Dr. Lathrop's assistant.

ELENA: What a pope cannot fix surely a cardinal cannot mend?

LAWRENCE: We mustn't get excited. We'll be up and around in no time.

ELENA: We! Is there something the matter with you?

LAWRENCE: I am using the invalid we.

ELENA: I *am* up and around. I'm simply lying here for the sake of the examination.

LAWRENCE: And that cane?

ELENA: I tripped over a daisy chain at the Vassar reunion of 1909. I sued successfully and created a Chair of Poetry.

LAWRENCE: I see. And it still gives you trouble?

ELENA: The chair?

LAWRENCE: No, the ankle.

ELENA: Sharpen your syntax, boy. Your credentials?

LAWRENCE: You'll have to take me on faith. I am Dr. Lathrop's assistant.

ELENA: What is your name?

LAWRENCE: Dr. Lawrence Hawley. Internist.

ELENA: Warren never mentioned an assistant. All these years. Don't you have a little card or something?

LAWRENCE *(Getting out wallet)*: I have a Diner's Card.

ELENA: You eat out? *(Aside)* The barbarism of the young! *(SHE looks at card.)*

LAWRENCE *(Taking card back)*: Are you satisfied?

ELENA: A meal ticket is not the same as a diploma. You look . . . reasonable . . . .

LAWRENCE: I think I may say, without false modesty, that I am the most careful physician in New York. A man I examined ten years ago is still waiting for the results of his blood test. *(Slight pause)* We've been in constant touch, of course.

ELENA: That is *some*thing of a recommendation. What is your specialty?

LAWRENCE: The liver. Without even examining you, I can tell your digestion of fats is a melancholy business.

ELENA: My dear man! Except for pastry, I have not touched a drop of fat in twenty years.

LAWRENCE: Ah, but pastry! The Vienna weakness! And the most insidious of foods! What you deny yourself with one hand, you imbibe with the other . . . *(Suddenly)* Do you really have a charge account at the New York Hospital?

ELENA: A place of refuge after one has been begrimed at Bloomingdale's.

LAWRENCE: Surely you had some specific symptom in mind when you called Dr. Lathrop?

ELENA: I have a stab in my back. Of course, I've been seeing *people*.

LAWRENCE: A desperate, if necessary measure. What sort of people?

ELENA: What sort of people would *you* recommend?

LAWRENCE: Calm, stimulating people.

ELENA: The calm ones aren't stimulating and the stimulating ones are crazy.

LAWRENCE: Maybe a month in the country would do you some good. Or a trip south.

ELENA: You have just described the poles of my repugnance. The country is full of snakes and the south southerners.

LAWRENCE: You asked for my advice.

ELENA: I asked for a small recommendation, not a total vision. I get *my* visions from the other world. Spirits, angels, demons . . .

LAWRENCE: You don't mean seances?

ELENA: I do.

LAWRENCE: How absurd!

ELENA: They are not absurd. They keep me in touch with the possible and they pass time. It seems to me everyone firstrate is dead. I'm lonely.

LAWRENCE: Then perhaps you should get away from the house, go out . . .

ELENA: Out? And what do you think out is? There's the street, the wretches who walk up and down on it, and a few trees. I exempt dogs because I am fond of them. But it is too dreary to be told to go out as if out were some sort of paradise. I've *been* out, and I don't like it.

69

The Folding Green

LAWRENCE: You're spoiled and childish.
ELENA: Spoiled and childish? I am merely discriminating. [*LAWRENCE takes out a stethoscope.*] Ah, what a charming case! It folds and it's green. [*SHE examines it.*] May I have it copied?
LAWRENCE: Why not? It's a gift from Vienna.
ELENA: Some of our spirits come from there. Freud, Mozart . . . the old gang.
LAWRENCE (*Primly*): The function of the liver is not a spiritual matter.
ELENA: You have an unsubtle mind.
LAWRENCE: And you have an undisciplined one. I am interested in facts, not nonsense.
ELENA: And what is a fact? The circumference of the world is twenty-five thousand miles. That doesn't tell us very much about the world.
LAWRENCE: But it tells us something. What is more factual than a human body? (*Contemptuously*) Do angels and spirits have bodies?
ELENA: They may appear as bodies. That's all *we*'re doing. The fact that the body exists doesn't make me certain it is the center of reality.
LAWRENCE (*Remembering who he is*): I don't have time for idle speculation. I am a diagnostician, not a philosopher.
ELENA: You haven't examined me and yet you've made a diagnosis. Actually, I haven't had very much pastry at all. I practically live on champagne.
LAWRENCE: And where do you get your protein?
ELENA: Oh, I nibble here and there. I have always been partial to snippets. Delicious little dribs and drabs.
LAWRENCE: And your digestion, doesn't it suffer?
ELENA: My digestion is splendid. I am all respiratory and lower back, I'm afraid. I seem to be a melting pot for the world's minor diseases.
LAWRENCE: Microbes are not able to distinguish one host from another.

Act One

ELENA: I had a little trouble myself when I used to go out.

LAWRENCE: The most extraordinary people are prey to the same bacteria that gorge themselves on the common horde. It is a little lesson in democracy.

ELENA: If you wait long enough, every expensive doctor will mention the word democracy. I assume, being an assistant, you are not as expensive as Warren.

LAWRENCE: We charge the same fees. House calls are extra.

ELENA: But in the word assistant, surely some hierarchy is implied. Since you are on a lower rung of the ladder, I should think you'd knock off a zero or two. Warren's nurse seems to add them arbitrarily to my bills.

LAWRENCE: It shocks me to discuss fees with the world's reputedly richest woman.

ELENA: It shouldn't. Who's more interested in money than the people who have it? It becomes an obsession. I speak in the general. As for me, I simply do not like to be cheated.

LAWRENCE: How will you ever know unless we start? The examination is beginning. Lie back.

ELENA: I *am* lying back.

LAWRENCE: Breathe.

ELENA *(Taking a deep breath)*: And what medical school did you say you went to?

LAWRENCE: Cornell.

ELENA: Ah, the white cliffs of 68th Street. And you interned?

LAWRENCE: Cough.

ELENA: That's where the vibration is.

LAWRENCE: Vibration?

ELENA: A sort of tingle-tangle that comes in the night and repeats and repeats . . .

LAWRENCE: Here?

ELENA: Close. You interned in an ambulance?

LAWRENCE: I have been in an ambulance. Say Ahh.

ELENA: Ahh. Rushing from one emergency to another?

LAWRENCE: Do you cough in the mornings?

ELENA: One must not cough too violently before eleven. By noon, I allow myself a small hack or two.

LAWRENCE: How about sleep? Do you sleep well?

ELENA: The few people who have seen me asleep have made favorable comments.

LAWRENCE: And you wake refreshed?

ELENA: Sometimes yes, sometimes no. Of course, that day will come when I will not wake at all.

LAWRENCE: I am here to stave off that inevitable event. [*HE twists ELENA's arm behind her back. She doesn't blanch.*] You seem in very good shape to me.

ELENA: You doctors never find anything wrong and you're so expensive going about it.

LAWRENCE: I am a scientist, not a poet . . .

ELENA: Alas!

LAWRENCE: I can only find what there is to find. Besides, doesn't being well make you happy?

ELENA: One doesn't hire musicians unless one wants them to play.

LAWRENCE: You're perfectly fine, you can get up, go out . . . I mean, stay in . . . do anything you want, within reason . . .

ELENA: Actually, I wanted to discuss something major with Warren. That's why I called.

LAWRENCE: Feel free. I had a whole semester in psychiatry.

ELENA: You see I've invited my daughter, my son-in-law, a few friends . . . How can I explain it to a mind so . . . so brackish?

LAWRENCE: Yes?

ELENA: Come into the study. My daughter and son-in-law are snooping about somewhere and my companion is the busiest busybody in town. You see, it's my will . . .

Act One

LAWRENCE: I'm a great believer in will.

ELENA: I mean, whom shall I leave my money to? I'm a lonely old woman, rich beyond the wildest dreams of avarice, and I dislike practically everyone. I can't die intestate. Half the world would grind to a stop.

LAWRENCE: Why don't you set up a foundation?

ELENA: Foundations consist of untalented people revenging themselves on the talented. No. I've thought of a scheme . . . and I need your help.

LAWRENCE: A scheme? What sort of a scheme?

ELENA: Come with me. Into the study. [*They walk toward study door. ELENA opens door. Just before they enter.*] You see, I want to play dead for three days.

[*LAWRENCE stands a moment, astonished, then follows ELENA into the study. As the study doors close, CORA and DONALD enter from side of stage opposite to study door.*]

DONALD: I really don't understand why we're here. What's the crisis?

CORA: How should I know? That telegram was the first I'd heard from her in fifteen years. You know we never see each other.

DONALD: Your fight with your mother is ancient history. I forgave her long ago.

CORA: You didn't have much to forgive. I can't forget she broke my father's heart. She wouldn't touch Barbridge's Frozen Foods—his passion, his monument . . .

DONALD: You talk about him as if he were a genius.

CORA: He was. He made apathy commercial. She could have tried one little French fried potato, for God's sake. Elena's always been impossible. She used to be really dreadful at the opening nights of the Opera.

DONALD: Wasn't everyone?

CORA: She had printed cards made up with grades on them, like A, B plus, and C. And she would go around giving people marks for their deportment. Once, she came right up to me and gave me a D minus in the middle of "Tristan." I still can't hear the "Liebestod" without going to pieces.

DONALD: "Tristan"? That's the one where the man's part is in German and the woman's in Italian, isn't it?

CORA: Yes.

DONALD: And the other parts?

CORA: There aren't any. It was a real love affair.

DONALD: Oh. Well. In all fairness, maybe your mother was trying to make some sort of point.

CORA: Point? Her behavior is the point. She didn't *have* to go to the Opera.

DONALD: And we didn't have to come here. Those bunk beds in the maid's room are humiliating.

CORA: Our time will come. I wouldn't *be* here if the telegram hadn't said something about changing her will. You know how much cold cash might be involved.

DONALD: We have plenty as it is.

CORA: You can stew in our little puddle of gold. I want a whole sea of it.

DONALD: The trouble is not that we're just a little rich. You're more than just a little greedy.

CORA: I have an idea. You know Felicity, Elena's ward—that little ape got up as Cinderella that we met last night?

DONALD: Yes. She's unforgettable.

CORA: Well, obviously she's closest to Elena's heart. She simpers around Elena like a trained toady. I'm sure Elena would leave her everything. But there's one chance.

DONALD: What's that?

ELENA: Felicity's stupid. BUT. She knows a great deal. A great deal I'd like to know.

DONALD: But if she's stupid, what could she know?

CORA: She's not really stupid, stupid. She plays the innocent with Elena. And you can't be innocent without being stupid. *You* can find out.

DONALD: Find out what? How?

CORA *(Very casually)*: You're an attractive man. There must have been *some* reason I married you.

Act One

DONALD: You don't mean ...

CORA: Everyone's a virgin for just so long. You'd be surprised at what virgins will tell their seducers. They get all gushy with confidences.

DONALD: Me seduce Felicity?

CORA: I'm not going to put it into coarse words. I've given you a hint.

DONALD: But she looks about twelve! When we arrived last night, she curtsied!

CORA: The debutante's reflex.

DONALD: I want to go back to Cleveland. A little golf, a little gin—that's good enough for me.

CORA: Come upstairs. I want to talk to you. I don't feel comfortable in this room. That companion of hers is always sneaking around.

DONALD: Back to those bunk beds?

CORA: We'll have a little after-lunch lunch. A little after-lunch-on-a-tray drink. On two levels—mine and yours.

DONALD: Felicity! I don't know if I can do it. Jail bait's never been my line.

CORA: You know I hate vulgarity even when it's masked as bawdy. Felicity's a very attractive girl. In a small way. [*The study door is opened from inside. Sounds of movement, voices.*] Hurry up! Someone's coming!

[*CORA and DONALD exit. A second later, ELENA and LAWRENCE emerge from the study.*]

ELENA: ... and so she became socially implausible from the neck up. Margaret suffered the most. I, of course, tried to do what I could, but Irma became increasingly intractable. So much so that Helga called in professional help. It was Henry finally who broke the news ... I must say Madeline was stoic, though less can be said for Millicent ... Audrey, on the other hand ...

LAWRENCE: I wish I were sure I was doing the right thing.

ELENA: Nonsense. It's all settled. And now let's celebrate! Ramona! [*RAMONA enters.*] Dr. Hawley is staying for lunch.

Throw another noodle on the chow mein.

RAMONA: We're not having chow mein today. Felicity thought the soy sauce was a bottle of ink and spoiled a day's correspondence.

ELENA: And spared us an ignoble Chinese dish. What are we having?

RAMONA: Prosciutto, Rabbit Agro Dolce, and Pintade Rotie. I forget the sequence.

ELENA: Use the diamond service.

RAMONA *(Stage whisper to ELENA)*: Who's the *rêve bateau?*

ELENA: Oh. My companion, Miss Kimono, Dr. Hawley.

LAWRENCE: How do you do.

RAMONA: I'm in the little room down the hall, Dr. Hawley. I have the strangest pain, sort of . . .

ELENA: That will be all, Ramona.

RAMONA: . . . acute, almost undiagnosable something, half dull wrack, half splintering headache . . . two doors down . . .

ELENA *(Emphasized)*: That . . . will . . . be . . . all.

[*RAMONA exits.*]

LAWRENCE: What's the matter with her?

ELENA: She can't decide whether she wants to be anonymous or immortal. Have some sherry, Dr. Hawley.

LAWRENCE: It will make me light-headed.

ELENA *(Pouring sherry)*: Lunch will anchor you again. Dr. Pointard was here yesterday. He's doing some brilliant things with cholesterol.

LAWRENCE: Pointard! Do you know him?

ELENA *(Stage laugh)*: Know him! He was my third lover. And he would have been my second if I hadn't got sidetracked at a stamp exhibit.

LAWRENCE: From what I read, I assumed you and your husband were supremely happy.

ELENA: Happy. But not supremely. Monogamy is the first refuge of the unattractive.

Act One

LAWRENCE: And the last?

ELENA: Morality. *(Loudly)* Ramona! The book! [*RAMONA enters with a stenographer's notebook and takes down what ELENA says in shorthand.*] *(Very fast)* Monogamy is the first refuge of the unattractive. And the last? Morality. *(To LAWRENCE)* I keep a little volume of epigrams. [*RAMONA exits.*]

LAWRENCE: It looks distressingly slim.

ELENA: A testament to its quality. It's the only reference book I use. [*Doorbell rings.*] That must be Teresa. She's doing a portrait of me pinned under a dragon. The sittings recapitulate the entire history of Christian martyrdom. [*JOHN enters.*]

JOHN: Miss Teresa Jones. [*JOHN exits. TERESA enters.*]

TERESA *(Embracing ELENA)*: My poor, dear, sick, darling. When I think of what *you* think you've been through . . .

ELENA: Miss Jones, Dr. Hawley.

TERESA and LAWRENCE: Hello.

TERESA: Has Warren taken one of his own prescriptions?

ELENA: He's in Hawaii.

TERESA: The land of leis! Do you travel, Dr. Hawley?

LAWRENCE: I've been to Venice.

TERESA: How nice! And did you like it?

LAWRENCE: It was one bacchanal* after another.

TERESA: A wit and a physician! Sit over here. [*LAWRENCE sits next to TERESA.*]

ELENA: He wasn't so witty when he arrived. It seems to have grown on him.

LAWRENCE: That's true. Mrs. Barbridge is a very bad influence on me.

TERESA: That's what the rich are for. I've never known a public benefactor who wasn't a private corrupter.

ELENA: I don't know why *you* say that.

---

*Pronounced "back canal."

The Folding Green

TERESA: I put five dollars in frozen soup last year and nothing's happened. I haven't made a penny.

ELENA: You get everything wrong. Frozen shrimp is where the real money is.

TERESA: Shrimp? I thought you said soup. You know, I'm starved. Turpentine makes me ravenous.

ELENA: Something special is being gassed in the kitchen. My food is always late. My cook cheats me unmercifully. Not that I can do anything about it . . .

LAWRENCE: Why not?

ELENA: I promised his father—my first lover—that I'd take care of him forever. And forever goes on and on. It's shocking the responsibility promiscuity thrusts on one.

TERESA: Promiscuity is the thief of time.

ELENA: Ramona! The book! [*RAMONA enters, scribbles, exits.*]

TERESA: Are you sure this cook is not a natural child? He seems to have a strange power over you.

ELENA: I'm really not sure. I moved much faster in the old days.

LAWRENCE: It shocks me to think you were immoral, Mrs. Barbridge . . .

TERESA: And it stupefies me to think you didn't keep count.

ELENA: A count once kept me. But that is neither here nor there. In the summer of 1910, I became fond of a crew member on a cruise. On luxury liners, the crew are infinitely more satisfactory than the passengers. Rounding the Horn, I was lured into the bowels of the ship for a game of Russian Bank. We lived in Paris together for three years.

LAWRENCE: Who?

ELENA: This stoker and I. Can't you follow a simple anecdote?

TERESA: But surely you would know if you had a child by him.

ELENA: The heat in the boiler room was terrific. Our

Act One

passion cooled in Paris. Though I can still remember the stale smell of champagne corks, the spell of ancient assignations. I'm sure there was a child somewhere. If it isn't this cook, it's someone equally well-placed.

TERESA: Well, after lunch, we must get back to the portrait. I'm very excited about it. It's green on green so nothing shows through.

ELENA: The more I look at it the more convinced I am that it's a still-life.

TERESA: Some people turn into still-lifes. Is that my fault?

ELENA: Still-lifes are not in the habit of paying a commission.

TERESA: Actually, for a few thousand more, I *could* make it look like you.

ELENA: I wonder. And how is Hoboken working out?

LAWRENCE: Hoboken?

TERESA: I'm painting Hoboken from every conceivable angle: at dawn, from a roof, at dusk, from a terrace . . . I fold in some green and I paint away. The old hotels are in ruins, the port is deserted. From the window of my loft . . . *(To LAWRENCE)* You *must* come and see me—I gaze down on twenty-four bars, each catering to seamen of a different nationality: Spanish, Greek, Honduran . . .

ELENA: The unions have ruined shipping and the theatre. That's why there are no showboats any more.

LAWRENCE: I've been looking for a painting for my office . . . something serene. What sort of things do you do?

TERESA: On weekdays, I'm a Neo-Fauvian Action-Magic Realist. On weekends, I paint what I think.

ELENA: Huge, uncluttered canvases.

TERESA *(To LAWRENCE)*: I'd *love* to do something for you. I have a "Rape of the Sabines." It's somewhat large. You have to look at it for years to find out what anyone is doing. You know, Elena, instead of a piddling commission, why don't you give me a grant? Something stupendous.

79

ELENA: Why?
TERESA: It would mean so little to you.
ELENA: Then why do it?
TERESA: For Art.
ELENA: Art has gotten along for centuries without me. I wouldn't dream of interfering now.
TERESA: You could support me and not interfere.
ELENA: No. I'm too intelligent to want to interfere and too discriminating not to. Besides, when one gives money away, one is despised for not giving more.
TERESA: The Duchess of Alba is remembered not for herself but because Goya painted her.
ELENA: You're painting me. Let's wait and see. It will be posterity and not our opinions which decide... [*RAMONA enters.*]
RAMONA: ... our opinions *that* decide ...
ELENA: If I had known she was a grammarian when the agency sent her, I never would have hired her. I asked for a gypsy who could type, and look what I got.
RAMONA: You know my shorthand is exquisite. Lunch is simmering to a draw. [*RAMONA exits.*]
ELENA: I made the mistake of having her educated. It cost me a small fortune in primers. And she tipples. Vast quantities of Cointreau. But she's worth it. I wouldn't say this in front of her, but her shorthand *is* exquisite. Everything she does has the quality of an illuminated manuscript. And she has remarkable extrasensory perception... [*FELICITY enters.*] Hello, darling. *(To others)* Felicity is the victim of every mailing list in the world. How many today, angel?
FELICITY: Two hundred and four!
ELENA: What busy scribblers everywhere! Anything interesting?
FELICITY: Another dual selection from the Fruit-of-the-Month Club.
ELENA: And the dividend?

Act One

FELICITY: One fruit fly. That is, one fruit fly when I opened the package. There are probably a million by now. [*FELICITY exits.*]

ELENA: Drosophila. *So* Mendelian.

TERESA: Where's she going now?

ELENA: To answer her second-class mail. She's searingly conscientious.

LAWRENCE: Charming creature. Who is she?

ELENA: Oh, I'm sorry. Felicity's my ward. And an orphan. The surviving child of my dead sister's ex-husband's marriage to his dead first wife.

TERESA: Were they all in an explosion or something?

ELENA: It was a *ménage à trois* that went down on the *Titanic*.

LAWRENCE: But she looks so young!

ELENA: Her parent had her at the very last possible minute. [*RAMONA enters and strikes a gong. It should be large, heavy, and get her into a lot of trouble.*] Is luncheon ready?

RAMONA: Most of it. Two eggs refused to separate.

ELENA: I admire loyalty even among the invertebrates. Well, help me in, somebody.

LAWRENCE: Really, Mrs. Barbridge, you can walk as well as I can.

ELENA: That's not good enough. [*LAWRENCE helps ELENA to dining-room door. TERESA pours herself another drink. They become separated momentarily. RAMONA leans over to hear conversation between LAWRENCE and ELENA.*]

LAWRENCE *(Stage whisper)*: I hope I'm not making a hideous mistake.

ELENA: It will not be the first in the history of medicine.

LAWRENCE: As a physician, I must point out that your cane is utterly superfluous.

ELENA: It's in keeping. We are about to have an utterly superfluous, utterly Italian meal. Even the ground glass is Venetian.

LAWRENCE: Sometimes, Mrs. Barbridge, I fear for you.

The Folding Green

ELENA: There is nothing to fear but nothing itself.

JOHN *(Entering and opening dining-room door)*: Luncheon, such as it is, is served.

[*All disappear into the dining room. CORA and DONALD enter.*]

CORA *(Looking at dining-room door)*: They're probably having something marvelous in there. And for us, tuna fish salad sandwiches on a tray.

DONALD: Take it easy. Revenge is a dish best eaten cold.

CORA: I think we may have just eaten it. [*Dining-room doors are flung open. ELENA emerges, supported by LAWRENCE. She totters about in a stagey way. They are followed by TERESA and FELICITY.*] What is it? What's the matter?

ELENA *(Clutching at her heart)*: My islands of Langerhans! Oh!

LAWRENCE: Steady, my dear.

DONALD: Can I help?

LAWRENCE: No, I'll take her to the hospital in my car. The less fuss the better.

CORA *(To TERESA)*: What happened?

TERESA: I don't know. It was so sudden. [*LAWRENCE exits with ELENA.*] And odd. She simply turned green, and folded.

TERESA: And slumped right over her prosciutto.

FELICITY: It was so delicious, too.

CORA: Has she been ill?

FELICITY: I think she's been working too hard on her will.

CORA: What about the will?

FELICITY *(Vague)*: She often spoke of you.

CORA: Oh, did she! You know a will can always be contested, especially by blood relatives.

TERESA: My lawyer was telling me something interesting about that the other day. He said that a dear old friend sometimes could make an equal claim. It's odd that you and Elena

Act One

haven't seen each other in fifteen years.

FELICITY: She often spoke of the Ashberrys, but I wouldn't want to repeat those horrible words.

DONALD: We might as well make it clear that unless we get the lion's share...

FELICITY: The lion's share is all. I mean it isn't the biggest piece, it's everything.

CORA: And I think it's even odder that you've become so informed in the last few minutes. You've been playing on my mother's sympathies for years, pretending to be a little wood sprite. Now, it turns out, you're practically Webster. Very peculiar.

FELICITY: She may not be dead yet, you know. [*Doorbell. JOHN enters.*]

JOHN: Madame Postova. [*JOHN exits. ELENA, disguised as a Russian noblewoman of the nineteenth century, enters. She should, of course, be recognizable to the audience as ELENA. Hat, muff, boots, etc.*]

CORA: Madame *Postova?*

ELENA *(Accent)*: I am a long lost cousin of Elena de Cordovan Barbridge. Beside myself with grief at the thought of her impending death, I flew over from Leningrad, formerly St. Petersburg.

DONALD: But she just became ill!

ELENA: A premonition forced me to the airdrome.

CORA: I never heard of any cousin.

ELENA *(Sitting down)*: What memories of other years! Ah, I recall too much of the past and too painfully!

DONALD: You knew Elena ... when?

ELENA: I came upon her first in a room at the Winter Palace crouched over an Ediphone set, her mouth slack with grief. Even then, she was trying to get in touch with the West. It was ... let me think ... 1873. I am very old.

DONALD: But that's practically a hundred!

ELENA: In Russia we live clean.

DONALD: And you haven't been in touch since?

The Folding Green

ELENA: Every Monday, I would send off sparks in the air. My sparks for Elena, I'd say. Across the earth. Across the sea.
CORA: And did anything catch fire?
ELENA: Mock an old woman, if you will! The young are cynical, ignorant . . . We would listen to music together. It was her passion. We would have risked Siberia for music, a little music . . .
CORA: There's no music here.
ELENA: And then, one day, she was gone. They took away my dearest thing. I was a Princess, you see . . . They separated us in 1899. The cruelty of Czars! And now!
FELICITY: Won't you take off your muff and scarf?
ELENA: Gentle Elena, how I shall miss her! What I would not give to see those dark eyes of hers once more, as bottomless as an ancient bidet! [*Doorbell. JOHN enters.*]
JOHN: Dr. Lawrence Hawley [*JOHN exits. LAWRENCE enters.*]
LAWRENCE: You must all prepare yourselves for a shock.
TERESA: She's worse!
LAWRENCE: Worse than that. She's dead.
ELENA: Agh, she is tasting the wafer of eternity!
CORA *(Just managing to get it out)*: Mother!
LAWRENCE *(As if recalling a great line)*: The last thing she said was, "Give my chickens feed."
FELICITY: How sweet!
ELENA: Dear old thing!
CORA: Where's the money?
LAWRENCE: She made an odd request at the end. There's a preliminary will. It sets up conditions which must be met before the final will can be read.
CORA: What! I don't understand.
LAWRENCE: Let me read it to you. *(Takes out papers, etc.)* To my loved ones behind me. Each of you must be dressed in a particular costume at the reading of my will. Costumes have been left in the attic for this purpose. *(To others)* There's a sealed envelope for each one of you, telling

Act One

you what you're supposed to be. There's also one for a Madame Postova.

FELICITY *(To ELENA)*: Elena must have suspected you'd be coming.

ELENA: She could read my thoughts across a thousand miles of tundra!

CORA: This is so typical of her. All this mumbo jumbo. She never did anything straight if she could mess it up a bit. Dressing up! Let me see that will!

[*LAWRENCE hands it to her. All the characters cluster round her, reading the will over her shoulder. ELENA leads LAWRENCE down to the footlights. The lights go out behind them, so that the other characters become invisible.*]

ELENA: Dr. Hawley, isn't it all working splendidly?

LAWRENCE: What a ridiculous get-up!

ELENA: It's an exact copy of Madame Arkadin's costume at the premiere of "The Sea Gull" in St. Petersburg on October 17, 1896. So it's authentic.

LAWRENCE: It looks silly on you. *(Suddenly, triumphantly, holding her away from him at arm's length)* I see you're not using your cane, Mrs. Barbridge!

ELENA: Dr. Hawley, what use are canes to the dead?

CURTAIN

The Folding Green

ACT TWO

SCENE ONE

SCENE: *The attic. A few days later. Stage is bare except for props mentioned in text. As each scene ends, there is a blackout followed by the immediate lighting of the next scene.*

AT RISE: *FELICITY, dressed as an angel, is busily working at her desk. On it there is the usual desk clutter, pens, including a plumed one, and a toy typewriter. Mail is scattered about.*

FELICITY: Dear. Dear? How do you spell "dear"? *(She takes out a dictionary, thumbs through it.)* ". . . dead, deaf, deal . . . dear." *(She types four strokes on her toy typewriter, then sits back and thinks.)* ". . . Amalgamated Mud, I was very pleased to know that . . ." No. "Dear Sirs, the fact that your mud is doing so well fills my heart . . ."
[DONALD *enters dressed as a pirate.*]
DONALD: Prepare to disembark, Felicity!
FELICITY *(Turning around)*: Ooh, you scared me! What are you supposed to be?
DONALD *(Disappointed)*: You mean you can't tell?
FELICITY: Let me think. Something to do with the sea?
DONALD: You're getting warm. Look at the crossbones. Look at the hat.
FELICITY: It rings a bell. I just can't . . . a lifeguard?
DONALD *(Giving up)*: No. I'm a pirate.
FELICITY: Of course! If I didn't know you, I would have got it right away. I mean the first thing I thought was: it's Cora's husband.
DONALD: Don't put too much stock in that, angel.

Act Two

FELICITY: You guessed! Actually, I don't have too much stock. My investments are all in this little green folder.

DONALD: What's all that stuff you're writing?

FELICITY: It's my mail. I write and write and it keeps coming . . . *(Showing him one after the other)* The Home Dentistry Club, Americans Divided for Action, National Rat Week . . .

DONALD: You mean you *answer* them?

FELICITY *(Surprised)*: Of course. They write to me. Don't *you* answer your mail?

DONALD: Yes, but not the stuff that just comes to the house! *(Getting on with it)* You know, you really look like an angel.

FELICITY: The wings aren't right. I stood on my bed and jumped and nothing happened.

DONALD: Well, what did you expect?

FELICITY: A little bounce or something.

DONALD: Bounce, eh? How's about a little kiss?

FELICITY: I never drink. Elena won't let me.

DONALD: Kiss, not drink. You're not a minor, are you?

FELICITY *(Coy)*: What do *you* think?

DONALD: Do you have any boyfriends?

FELICITY: I had one. But I had to give him up.

DONALD: Why?

FELICITY: Every time I looked in his eyes, I saw two small Chinese restaurants.

DONALD: Here, look in my eyes. What do you see?

FELICITY *(Shrinking back, after looking)*: It's too horrible to say.

DONALD: Come on. We're not children.

FELICITY: No. I just can't.

DONALD: Please, you're hurting my feelings. What did you see?

FELICITY: All right. Cora.

DONALD *(Impatiently)*: Forget about her.

FELICITY: But she's your wife.

87

DONALD: Well, I'll tell you. After a certain point in marriage—about twenty seconds, I'd say—you realize you need to broaden your experience. You say to yourself: "Goodbye, fidelity."

FELICITY: That's not my name. It's Felicity.

DONALD *(Changing tack)*: You know, you haven't paid much attention to me.

FELICITY: I have all my mail to answer. And I'm upset about Aunt Elena's not having a funeral. We can't even go to the cremation. Why wasn't there a funeral?

DONALD: It doesn't seem like Elena not to have had one. It should have been a vast undertaking... You know, you're sweet.

FELICITY: Am I? I'm a very ordinary girl. I just bang away up here.

DONALD: How about a little hug?

FELICITY: Maybe. Maybe it would unlock my creative powers.

DONALD *(Embracing her)*: You *are* an angel!

FELICITY: Watch my wings! [*DONALD kisses FELICITY passionately.*] Was that sex?

DONALD: It was as close as you can come without landing on the other side. [*FELICITY kisses DONALD passionately, turning him as horizontal as possible.*] Hey, wait a minute!

FELICITY *(Hoarse stage whisper)*: Where does she keep the bonds?

DONALD: What bonds?

FELICITY: The Russian Imperial.

DONALD: I was going to ask you.

FELICITY: They went through the Swiss bank. They just look like Russian Imperial Bonds. It's all the frozen food money—as if you didn't know! I have a little scheme.

DONALD: No, no. I can't. I'm from Cleveland.

FELICITY: Does Cora know where they are? Look. I'll split my half with you.

Act Two

DONALD: But supposing she leaves it all to Cora?
FELICITY: Don't be silly. At least half of it is mine. And she may cut Cora off completely. It won't work if Cora knows where the bonds are. They're transferrable, you idiot.
DONALD: But Cora thinks you . . . *(HE thinks twice about this.)* Where do *you* think they are?
FELICITY: There's a cabinet down in the cellar. I've worked at it for ten years and nothing gives.
DONALD: What about Ramona?
FELICITY: She doesn't know anything. It's Cora I'm worried about.
DONALD: But she's my wife. I'd get it anyway.
FELICITY: This way you're sure of half one way or the other. You see?
DONALD: And all this mail you answer? It's just a front?
FELICITY: A second front. I've been investing my little allowance in little companies around the world. Plexiglas. Magnesium. Hair tonic.
DONALD: Don't you get any personal mail?
FELICITY: What's that?
DONALD: I'm going to write you a letter, angel. A personal letter to an angel from a pirate.
FELICITY: And tonight you'll ask Cora? Subtly. Just say: "Do you know anything about the bonds?" Watch her reaction. And report to me.
DONALD: That's not very subtle.
FELICITY: For Cora, it'll do.
DONALD: And how about meeting me a little later tonight? When you're not an angel?
FELICITY *(Prim again)*: I'm way behind schedule. I may have to stay up half the night. Amalgamated Mud declared a dividend. I'm reinvesting it in Canadian Rain.
DONALD: One good turn deserves another. We'll stay up together. I'll help you. You know the broom closet on the third floor? Behind the folding green shutters? I'll be there at eleven, waiting. A deal?

The Folding Green

FELICITY: How do you spell "deal"?
DONALD *(To FELICITY)*: "D...e...a..." *(To audience)* "d."
[*DONALD exits blowing FELICITY a kiss.*]
FELICITY: Men! They're all prigs! I mean pigs.
[*TERESA enters, dressed as a Spanish woman. She has a moth-eaten mantilla slung over her shoulders.*]
TERESA: What do you think of this mouldy rag? Will I get by as a Spanish noblewoman?
FELICITY: It's rather pretty.
TERESA: Even the moths wouldn't finish it. Do I look Castilian?
FELICITY: A little bit.
TERESA: Something tells me it's the cocktail hour. I always know. Put me in the remotest jungle, take away my watch, and I'll tell you exactly when the cocktail hour is taking place in every major city in the world.
FELICITY: Including Hoboken?
TERESA: Hoboken isn't a major city. It's one long bar disguised as a depressed area.
FELICITY: You know so many things! I don't seem to be able to do anything but answer my mail.
TERESA: It's a nice hobby.
FELICITY: Not as good as knowing when the cocktail hour is.
TERESA: It takes a lot of experience. I drank for twenty-five years before I could pin it down exactly. *(SHE takes out a flask.)* Have a warmish martini?
FELICITY: I don't drink. Aunt Elena said since I had no distinction she was determined to give me one.
TERESA: You're a virgin, aren't you.
FELICITY: I *think* so.
TERESA: I have a feeling you're not thinking hard enough. Here, try a slug.
FELICITY *(Taking a sip)*: It's odd, but fascinating.
TERESA: It's the great loophole of civilization. Have some

Act Two

more. [*FELICITY drains the flask.*] Beginners mustn't guzzle. How do you feel?
 FELICITY: Funny.
 TERESA: A little disoriented, eh? *(Takes out compact and starts to powder her nose.)* Tell me, Felicity, did you ever hear Elena say something about . . . bonds?
 FELICITY: She never discussed business with me. "You're such a harebrained little thing," she used to say. I do miss her so!
 TERESA: And she never mentioned the word "Imperial"?
 FELICITY: Imperial? I don't *think* so. Why?
 TERESA: Oh, it's just a crazy little theory of mine. Would you do me a favor, darling?
 FELICITY: Of course, if I can.
 TERESA: Would you go downstairs and tell John to send up some gin and vermouth? The one with the green label. You drank my last smidgeon.
 FELICITY: I'll go get it myself.
 TERESA: You're an angel. [*FELICITY exits.*]
 TERESA: Spain, Spain! Land of the mantilla, land of the flamenco . . . *(SHE puts her hands flat on the table.)* Land of the inquisition . . . *(The table begins to shake.)* What the . . . *(Smoke, etc.)* My God! [*FIGURE appears.*]
 FIGURE: Baron Rothschild. At your service, madame.
 TERESA: Rothschild! I thought all the Rothschilds were dead!
 FIGURE: A tasteless joke, madame.
 TERESA: Who *are* you?
 FIGURE: About the debentures, madame.
 TERESA: What debentures? I think you've come to the wrong . . .
 FIGURE: Convert the debentures, madame. That is my considered opinion. *(HE walks up to TERESA and takes one of her hands in his.)* What exciting protoplasm!
 TERESA: Please! Who *are* you?
 FIGURE *(Putting his arm around TERESA)*: Beautiful

skin!

TERESA: It's just . . . cell after cell.

FIGURE: I've always had a weakness for Spanish women. [*HE puts other arm around TERESA. He slowly embraces her and bends her backwards.*]

TERESA: But I'm not Spanish! [*HE pays no attention.*] My name is Jones!

FIGURE: Ah, you little devil! Jones indeed! [*FIGURE begins to seduce TERESA seriously. She struggles and cries out in alarm.*]

TERESA: How dare you! Help! [*RAMONA enters in a gypsy costume.*]

RAMONA *(Sees FIGURE)*: You! [*FIGURE hangs head in shame.*] What are you doing here?

TERESA *(To RAMONA)*: You know him! Who is he?

RAMONA: He's a . . . a hired entertainer. I've employed him myself on Elena's instructions.

TERESA: You've had entertainments! Why wasn't I invited?

RAMONA: They were private. *(Aside to FIGURE)* Dreg from Equity!

TERESA: His ideas of entertainment are very advanced. *(To FIGURE)* I ought to have you booked. Seducing a lady in the house of your employer.

FIGURE: I was rehearsing. There's this play by Don Luis de Gongora. I thought you were . . .

RAMONA: Get out!

FIGURE: You are an exquisite gypsy, madame. Incomparable artistry . . .

RAMONA: Leave! [*FIGURE starts toward exit. Stops.*]

FIGURE *(To RAMONA, by way of getting* something *in edgewise)*: By the way . . . we're out of smoke. [*FIGURE exits.*]

RAMONA: Actors, they're so eccentric. And hungry. And vain. I told Elena we never should have hired him. You'd better get ready. The will is going to be read in a matter of

Act Two

moments. [*RAMONA exits.*]
 TERESA: I need a drink! I thought he was a ghost. Ramona says he's an actor. She's a gypsy. I'm a Spaniard. Everything's topsy-turvy. [*FELICITY enters with gin and vermouth.*] There you are. [*TERESA pours gin and vermouth into a tumbler and whisks it around.*] Here, try one.
 FELICITY *(Drinking)*: To think! I found out what sex is and I'm having a martini all on the same day.
 TERESA: You're lucky! *(Slowly)* I ... found ... out ... at ... *night*.
[*Lights out. And immediately up on another part of the attic. DONALD, in pirate costume is doing a soft shoe routine. CORA as a Gibson girl is primping in front of a mirror.*]
 CORA: And so I said to my father: Why not put the Antarctic to some commercial use? There it is, congealing in the sun, and no one's doing a thing about it. Are you listening?
 DONALD: Mmn hmmn.
 CORA: So that's where he got the idea of taking the food to the tundra and freezing it up there. I was the first person in the world to throw a French fried potato onto an ice floe and watch it freeze. I can still hear the cheers of the laboratory technicians.
 DONALD *(In time to music)*: Da da bom!
 CORA: The most unforgettable character I ever met was my father. Guided by the star of his success, a colossus among pygmies, a beacon in the wilderness, he moved unfalteringly from the peak of one triumph to another: Green peas, Chicken a la King, Welsh rarebit ...
 DONALD: A razz ma tazz ...
 CORA: ... and various seeded fruits. "When you want to be assured of the best, buy Barbridge!" Don't you think that's the most beautiful line in all of poetry?
 DONALD: I *do* like "I scooped a tankard brewed in pearl." Or is it "I brewed a tankard stewed in oil"?
 CORA: Emily Dickinson ... that rotter! *(Laying down tools)* Are you prepared to defend me at the hearing?

DONALD: At great lengths.
CORA: Do you love me?
DONALD: Madly.
CORA: Even though you're going to sleep with Felicity for business purposes?
DONALD *(Stops)*: But isn't that what *we've* been doing?
CORA: No, no. We've been doing business together for sleeping purposes . . . We'd better get ready. [*Lights dim.*]
DONALD *(Advancing to footlights)*: Are you wearing your lamé?
CORA *(Advancing to footlights)*: I'll be wearing my lamé.
DONALD: You'll look gold in it again.
CORA: I'll look gold in it again. Are you wearing your bow tie?
DONALD: I'll be wearing my bow tie.
CORA: You'll look black and white again.
DONALD: I'll be black and white again.
CORA: With the studs?
DONALD: With the studs.
CORA: Lady Lip knows how to walk.
DONALD: And Lord Smear knows how to talk. [*Lights dim further.*]
CORA: I'm afraid in the dark.
DONALD: There is nothing in the dark.
CORA: Yes, there's something in the dark.
DONALD: What *is* there in the dark?
CORA: There's an end in the dark.
DONALD: Yes, there's *that* in the dark.
CORA: When the sun goes down . . .
DONALD: Yes, I'm afraid *then* . . .
CORA: Shall we dress in the dark?
DONALD: No address in the dark.
CORA: Shall we dress?
DONALD: Yes.

[*Lights immediately on. ELENA dressing. She is getting into a Marie Antoinette costume, with an enormously wide*

Act Two

skirt. *Eye mask on table. She dresses and makes up as scene proceeds. LAWRENCE enters.*]

LAWRENCE: Ah, there you are.

ELENA *(At mirror)*: I've never had much sympathy with Marie Antoinette. I hate women who lose their heads.

LAWRENCE: Then why choose her for your own impersonation?

ELENA: Because I've never lost mine. You learn something by anticipating what history has made unavoidable.

LAWRENCE: It must have been awful, that one moment on the guillotine.

ELENA: Who knows if it was one moment? It might have been a lifetime. I comfort myself with the knowledge that nothing is as terrible as the subsequent recollection of it.

LAWRENCE: Your costume's becoming.

ELENA: I have always tried to fit into a tradition. The point is in finding the right one. That's why I hate fashion. I believe one should dress as a Greek one day, an Elizabethan the next. And since they are all human, one is never likely to be wrong.

LAWRENCE: But one is likely to be in bad taste.

ELENA: There is no such thing as good and bad taste. There is merely taste and no taste. All clothes are an illusion. The costume I'm wearing wasn't a costume once.

LAWRENCE: Illusion, Mrs. Barbridge, dies on deathbeds.

ELENA: Along with everything else—depending on whether death is only another illusion. In any case, how dreary it would be if all our images had to be propped up by such really odiously vulgar supports as fact and actuality. Without illusion, I could not be giving this lavish masquerade.

LAWRENCE: The notion that it is lavish is merely another illusion.

ELENA: Precisely. Illusion steadies everything. That's why people drink: so as not to be themselves, or to be *more* themselves. A proper disguise does just as well. If you only knew how often people disguised themselves without being aware

of it! A costume simply makes the falsity of truth apparent.
LAWRENCE: Well, *I* don't have one.
ELENA: You don't need one. You're a doctor of internal medicine. The body—for you—is a disguise in itself.
[*JOHN enters.*]
JOHN: Passing through the living room a moment ago, I saw a pirate, a Gibson girl, and something resembling a Spanish woman.
ELENA: Where's Felicity?
JOHN: Dressing and undressing.
ELENA: Ah! Her condition has at last caught up with her potentiality.
JOHN: They're all waiting for someone. Shall I say you'll be down, Madame Postova?
ELENA: In a moment.
[*JOHN exits.*]
LAWRENCE: Miss Jones has decided to do my portrait.
ELENA: Really? I hope it turns out better than mine.
LAWRENCE: She's going to use nothing but patent medicines.
ELENA: It's an idea so original that it leaves one with nothing to say.
LAWRENCE: Do you think Teresa would make a good wife?
ELENA: It will be the first thing she's ever made.
LAWRENCE: No, I mean it. Seriously.
ELENA: Seriously? She's fearfully sluttish and frightfully particular. She's selfish and self-interested. But her cruelty, like mine, is only a game. Make sure you want to play it, Lawrence.
LAWRENCE: That's the first time you've called me Lawrence. I'd find it difficult to say "Elena."
ELENA: Try.
LAWRENCE: Elena. I like Teresa. Very much.
ELENA: So I gather. (*SHE walks up to mirror. Stands in front of it a moment.*) Let them eat cake . . .

Act Two

LAWRENCE: That sounded imperial.

ELENA *(Casually)*: On the same day, I've been French and Russian. That's why I sound imperial. *(Gaily)* Dressing up *does* so free one from bonds. [*ELENA exits.*]

LAWRENCE *(Rising, looking after her. Slowly)*: Russian. Imperial. Bonds.

CURTAIN

ACT TWO

SCENE TWO

SCENE: *The living room. Immediately following.*

AT RISE: *CORA, DONALD, TERESA, FELICITY, in costume, are seated, drinking.*

TERESA: I feel absolutely irrepressible tonight. I have a notion something tremendous is about to happen.

DONALD: You seem more like yourself, oddly, in costume.

TERESA: Being odd, I am more like myself oddly.

FELICITY: Another double martini, please.

TERESA: I must say you're taking to that stuff.

FELICITY: I could kick myself for not having started earlier. Wasted years!

TERESA: Well, be careful. The next thing you know, you'll be smoking.

DONALD: My brokers called a moment ago. They're creating an artificial panic on the market. They're buying quantities of worthless common stock and unloading valuable shares of preferred. The automobile may soon be replaced by the garage as the dominant factor in the American economy. I now own sixty-four percent of all the garages in the Western Hemisphere.

CORA: *We* own.

DONALD: Sorry, dear. *We* own.

CORA: This Gibson girl costume is *hot*. I'm sweltering. All these folds.

TERESA *(To CORA)*: I'm green with envy. [*ELENA enters.*]

ELENA: My dears, I am very anxious . . .

TERESA: What a splendid get-up, Madame Postova!

ELENA: Thank you. I wanted to be inconspicuous. My

Act Two

dears. I am very anxious to hear Elena's will. Not for its contents—I am insupportably rich—but for its literary quality. I have always said, and to her face, too, that Elena was potentially a great writer.

TERESA: Everyone is, potentially. But as William Blake said, "Execution is the chariot of genius."

FELICITY: I think it's mean to mention "execution" in front of Marie Antoinette.

CORA: I'm not so sure of that. Perhaps if the word had been mentioned more often she might have avoided the actuality. [LAWRENCE enters.]

LAWRENCE: Mrs. Barbridge's lawyer is ill and so I will read the will in his place.

CORA: That seems very odd to me.

DONALD: To me, too.

ELENA: What's odd about it? Every day *some*body is ill.

LAWRENCE (Reading): "The last will and testament of Elena de Cordovan Barbridge, subject to a final will . . ."

CORA: Don't "last" and "final" mean the same thing?

TERESA: Oh, it's legal language. The words don't mean anything the first time, so they repeat them.

ELENA: Proceed.

LAWRENCE: "I leave my entire estate to the possessor of the Russ . . ." Damn it! This thing is backwards. *(He turns it around, upside down, then around again.)* "I, Elena de . . ." [As LAWRENCE begins above speech, WOMAN enters and walks up to ELENA.]

WOMAN: We were underpaid, madame.

ELENA: Who are you? *(To others)* Who is she? *(To WOMAN)* I don't know you.

WOMAN: Your companion cheated us, Mrs. Barbridge. My son and I . . .

CORA: Mrs. *Bar*bridge! [FIGURE enters.]

FIGURE: We are very sorry to interrupt, madame, but it's only fair . . .

WOMAN: You see, at the last seance, your companion gave

The Folding Green

us each forty dollars. We asked for fifty and she short-changed us. Someone owes us ten.
FIGURE: Apiece.
TERESA *(Slow dawn)*: You know, you look familiar.
FIGURE: I am happy to make your acquaintance, madame.
ELENA: Who *are* these creatures?
FIGURE: Don't you remember me? Look, my hood!
WOMAN: Look! My cape!
DONALD *(To ELENA)*: Who are *you?*
WOMAN: Why she's Mrs. Barbridge, of course. That is a superb disguise but it doesn't fool me, I'm a pro. I've been in the game for forty years. I have a fresco from Ionesco, a tray from Genet . . .
ELENA: Ramona.
[*RAMONA enters.*]
RAMONA *(To WOMAN and FIGURE)*: Get out! Both of you!
WOMAN *(To ELENA)*: But that is not your companion! That is a gypsy!
TERESA *(Looking closely at Marie Antoinette)*: Why, I think it *is* Elena!
DONALD: What the hell is going on here?
FIGURE: We're just trying to receive our just wages.
WOMAN: The fruit of our labor.
ELENA: Mrs. Barbridge. She dead.
WOMAN: We know you're rehearsing but *(hideous little laugh)* money is money. I hope, Mrs. Barbridge, we haven't upset . . .
RAMONA: This is a wake. Mrs. Barbridge is dead.
WOMAN: Well, then, who is that?
LAWRENCE: Please! Do you want to hear the will or not?
ELENA *(Tearing off eye shades)*: So the spirits were *hired!* I can't go on with this farce any longer.
TERESA: Just as I thought! Elena.
ELENA: You were right, Dr. Hawley. There are no spirits,

Act Two

after all.

DONALD: You mean this is all play-acting?

ELENA: I wanted you all to hear my will.

CORA: You mean you got us into these . . . these vestments as a joke?

ELENA: It took a great deal of planning.

TERESA: Well, I think it's a mess.

ELENA: Very few people realize how much planning it takes to make a mess.

CORA: I'm glad you're alive, mother.

DONALD: And I am, too.

ELENA *(To RAMONA)*: You!

RAMONA: I can explain. *(To WOMAN and FIGURE)*: Tell her how you needed a place to rehearse, how out of the kindness of my heart . . .

WOMAN: Yes, my son and I are trying out for a road company production of Ibsen's "Ghosts," and this kind lady . . .

CORA: And you paid them? To rehearse here? And I suppose the birds put out crumbs for *you*.

RAMONA: As a matter of fact . . .

ELENA: Please! *(To RAMONA)* Isn't it enough that you deceived me by hiring the spirits? Must we also have this bickering at the reading of my will? Pay them. [RAMONA *does.*]

WOMAN and FIGURE: Thank you, madame. *(To ELENA)* Thank *you*, madame. [*THEY exit.*]

ELENA *(To RAMONA)*: I'll attend to you later. My dears, there *is* a will. A real will. And I want to read it to you now. I see no point in your fighting over my money when I am no longer here to enjoy the fracas.

CORA: Can't I get out of this? I'm being strangled in acres of cheese cloth.

ELENA: No. We must be in costume.

DONALD: But why?

ELENA: Death puts everything in a new light. Costumes are a first step along the way. *(To DONALD)* Your Christian

name lasts only a lifetime, but piracy goes on forever.
  CORA: Then why are you Marie Antoinette? *She* didn't go on forever.
  ELENA: To remind myself that even queens are dragged to the market place.
  CORA: But she wasn't a queen!
  ELENA: All the more reason. She made the mistake of trying to be one. And now the will.
  LAWRENCE: What about *this* will?
  ELENA: A clue on the treasure hunt. *(Calling to wings)* John! The ladder! [*JOHN enters carrying a small aluminum ladder. He hands it to ELENA.*] Thank you.
  JOHN: Madame.
  [*ELENA takes ladder, walks over to back wall, where she leans ladder against book case, climbs up to rubber plant, lifts plant out of its pot, and takes out some papers. JOHN exits.*]
  RAMONA: The Russian Imperial! . . .
  ELENA: Here we are. *(SHE looks at RAMONA meaningfully, takes out a pair of scissors, and cuts out a paragraph or two which float to the floor.)*
  RAMONA: Oh, no! Elena! . . .
  ELENA *(From top of ladder)*: Here is my whole life tied up in a bunch of papers. Here is the last accolade or the slyest twist of the knife. What malice goes into wills, my dears! What disappointments, slights, and cheats are, in the end, revenged! And how many accidental kindnesses rewarded a thousand-fold! To the nurse who brought the syringe on time. To the gardener who coaxed the reluctant rose. But after the pets are cared for, and the eccentric philanthropies fattened on a whim, then, *then*, we get to the heart of the matter! Who loved us? Who despised us? I would not burden those who loved me with my fortune. Or honor those who despised me. Ah, but the indifferent! How the heart desires to win them over! When you make your wills, my children, beware of those who are not aware of you. Those who love us will love us no matter. Those who despise us we learn to despise. But

Act Two

those who do not care! One is tempted to leave them everything.

TERESA *(With great sincerity)*: I don't care.

[*ELENA starts to descend and ladder begins to wobble. She waves papers in the air to balance herself.*]

LAWRENCE: Elena, be careful!

[*But the ladder teeters and ELENA falls on the floor in a heap, the papers scattered around her.*]

DONALD: My God!

TERESA: Elena!

[*They all rush toward ELENA, but LAWRENCE gets there first and waves them aside. He kneels beside her and feels her pulse.*]

LAWRENCE *(After listening to her heart, etc. Slowly getting to his feet)*: She's dead. [*They all stand there, stunned. Finally...*]

TERESA: Are you sure this isn't another performance?

LAWRENCE: Alas, this time it's true. *(To DONALD)* Help me with her.

DONALD: Where will we put her?

LAWRENCE: On the settee in the dining room.

[*DONALD and LAWRENCE lift ELENA onto their shoulders and carry her off in a dead march.*]

RAMONA *(Picking up a piece of paper. Reads.)*: "I leave my book of epigrams to a crook in my employ."

CORA: You see, she didn't forget you.

RAMONA: Obviously she meant "cook in my employ." Wills are always full of typographical errors.

TERESA: We're not supposed to read that anyway. It's illegal. [*LAWRENCE and DONALD re-enter.*]

LAWRENCE *(To RAMONA)*: Give me that! *(Puts piece of paper back among others.)* Only Elena would have kept her will in a loose-leaf notebook. John is calling the coroner. Are we ready?

CORA: Unless at least half comes to me, I want to make it clear...

The Folding Green

LAWRENCE: Let us have a little respect for the dead. Silence. Quote. "I, Elena de Cordovan Barbridge, of the County of Manhattan, State of New York, do hereby make, publish and declare . . .
TERESA: Can't we skip all that junk?
LAWRENCE *(To others)*: Shall we skip all the junk?
EVERYONE: Yes.
LAWRENCE *(Reading)*: "I give, devise and bequeath . . . blah blah" Let's see. *(HE turns pages.)* "I bequeath to my daughter, Cora Ashberry, one jar of cold cream, one seat in perpetuum to the Chicago Opera, and my town house in New York."
CORA: And the money? Where's the money?
LAWRENCE: That's all there seems to be about you. "To my son-in-law, Donald Ashberry, I leave my seat on the New York Stock Exchange."
DONALD: I *have* a seat on the Exchange.
TERESA: Well, now you have two. You can buy and sell yourself blue.
LAWRENCE: Please! *(Reading)* "My income from the rural electrification of Africa may be used by Teresa Jones to take a trip around the world, provided she doesn't stop."
TERESA: Ever?
LAWRENCE: "All my oil, coal, gold, zinc, copper, iron, steel, wool, silk, lumber, glass, plastic, and leather holdings go to Felicity, my ward, in trust until she be ninety-five, whereupon the principal shall devolve to her. Dr. Lawrence Hawley receives a sustaining membership in the Museum of Modern Art." *(Bitterly to others)* I've *seen* all those movies.
TERESA: Did she mean I could never stop, not even overnight?
LAWRENCE: Oh, I'm sure she meant you could stop overnight.
TERESA: Thank God!
CORA: Cold cream!
TERESA: And the Chicago Opera, darling. Their "Lohen-

Act Two

grin" is supposed to be absolutely crackerjack.

LAWRENCE: Quiet, there's more. "The frozen shrimp egg roll money goes to my cook."

RAMONA: And me. What about me—her faithful companion for over twenty-five years?

LAWRENCE: I'm just coming to you—what's left of you, I mean. "Ramona Kimono, my companion . . ."

TERESA: I didn't know your last name was Kimono.

RAMONA: It's always been.

LAWRENCE: ". . . is appointed the head of a new foundation, 'The Institute for Spiritual Refinements.' " And there are a couple of paragraphs cut out. Then, quote, "The Institute, hers in perpetuity, has neither capital nor interest."

RAMONA: How mean! She cut me out at the last minute!

LAWRENCE *(Going on)*: "The profits from the sale of my personal jewelry shall be used to supply one copy of Proust in every hotel and motel room in the United States and Canada. I leave to the discretion of the Canadian authorities whether the copies in Quebec and Montreal shall be in English or in French."

CORA: Is there any more for us?

LAWRENCE *(Flipping through pages)*: There's some charity stuff . . .

TERESA *(Stretching her arms)*: I'm going around the world! Tahiti, Fiji, Bali . . .

CORA: You're stuck already.

LAWRENCE: You know, Teresa, I'm going around the world myself. What a coincidence!

TERESA: How divine! To have one's own physician in every port!

CORA: I don't think my mother meant for you to stop at all. I think she meant for you to keep going.

TERESA *(Ignoring this)*: Well, I don't think we came out too badly, knowing Elena. She might have left everything to a dog or something.

CORA: *Badly!* Who wants an opera seat, especially in a

The Folding Green

city I would rather *die* than be seen in?
TERESA: You have oodles of money as it is. What are you complaining about?
CORA: I'm going to sue.
TERESA: I wouldn't do that if I were you. I can remember quite clearly some remarks Elena made about you. They'd have a certain ring in a court room.
CORA: Don't threaten me, Miss Jones. You're lucky to have gotten anything. Felicity, that common drunk, has the bulk of the estate. No . . . wait a minute. Daddy's frozen food money! The Russian Imperial . . .
RAMONA: The Russian Imperial! . . . [*RAMONA exits.*]
LAWRENCE: Here's the second part. Quote. "My principal and *real* income goes to the holder of the Russian Imperial Bonds."
CORA: But where *are* they?
DONALD: We thought Felicity knew.
CORA *(To TERESA)*: And I think *you* know.
TERESA: And *I* think Ramona knows. Ramona! [*RAMONA enters.*]
CORA: Where are the bonds?
RAMONA: If I knew, I wouldn't be standing here absolutely penniless. I've nothing. And she promised me so much. What shall I do?
CORA: I don't even know where the pantry is in this barn of a house. Why don't you stay on for a while? You can cook for us . . .
RAMONA: Cook!
CORA: And now let's search this house inside out for those bonds.
LAWRENCE: *None* of you know where they are?
DONALD: Where the hell could she have put them? And what's the point of leaving money you can't get your hands on?
TERESA: Isn't that the way money is always left?
LAWRENCE: Here it is. Quote. "Secret Clause Number

Act Two

One. The Russian Imperial Bonds may be found in anything green that folds. I hid the folding green in the folding green. My little joke. Love, E."

CORA: And what does that mean?

DONALD *(Tentatively)*: Felicity has a green folder.

LAWRENCE: And the broom closet on the third floor. With the folding green doors! [*THEY all start impulsively for the doors.*]

RAMONA: And my dress! [*THEY stop.*]

CORA: You're out of it. You've been disinherited. *Cook.*

RAMONA: My dress has green folds. She probably sewed the bonds in. And no one's taken them out. So I still . . .

TERESA *(Pointing to CORA)*: But Cora's skirt must be made out of your old dress. Look! The green folds! The bonds are right there!

CORA: Scissors, here I come. [*THEY all rush out, leaving RAMONA onstage alone.*]

RAMONA: Fools! *(Walks over to bookcase, looks at spines of books.)* Ah, here it is! *(Reading title)* Folding by Henry Green: *The Murderer's Cook Book. (Takes it down from shelf, flips pages.)* "Truss the chicken and . . . " Trusses are so expensive! *(Flips pages.)* "Baked Alaska. Go to the North Pole. Focus the sun through a piece of isinglass . . ." Too hard! *(Flips pages.)* "Marinate the victim overnight in a mixture of jelly beans, kale, flageolets . . . " Flageolets! How cruel! The hell with this cook book! *(Throws it into wings, takes out stenographer's notebook, and writes as she speaks.)* "Ramona Kimono's Tomato Soup Surprise. Pour ketchup in hot water and serve." [*WOMAN and FIGURE enter quickly.*] You're late. There will be penalties.

WOMAN: We just got your cable.

RAMONA: I sent a telegram.

WOMAN: I know, but a water main burst on 59th Street. We slogged our way over.

RAMONA: Mrs. Barbridge is dead.

WOMAN *(Crossing herself)*: *Pax romana obfuscata mort.*

FIGURE: Ditto.
RAMONA: At least I *think* she's dead.
WOMAN: She's had her last resurrection. A grand woman. And so rich.
FIGURE: Billions, according to *Business Week*. And all we get is a mere pittance.
RAMONA: You're more than adequately paid, in my opinion, which happens to be the opinion that counts.
WOMAN: Let's get to the point. We want a third of whatever you get.
RAMONA *(Stage laugh)* A third! You must be mad!
WOMAN: Let me tell you a little story. I was walking past the D.A.'s office yesterday, and I was thinking, "I wonder what he'd have to say about a woman servant who fooled around with her dead mistress's fortune in some spiritualistic way." It just crossed my mind.
RAMONA: Allow me to uncross it. As far as *I* know, you were simply hired to lend a bit of credence to a passion of the late Mrs. Barbridge's—historical research through spiritualism.
WOMAN: Twenty percent.
RAMONA: *No* percent. And that's the last word on the subject. Because *I* wonder what the D.A. would think about a frump who lived in Miami for three months in the winter of 1962 pretending to be Mrs. Elena de Cordovan Barbridge.
WOMAN: I don't know what you're talking about!
RAMONA: Don't you—Minnie Turner Gravotsky?
WOMAN: How did you know?
RAMONA: I hired you to begin with because you'd impersonated Elena.
WOMAN *(To FIGURE)*: Did you tell her . . . fink?
FIGURE: Me!?
WOMAN: Let us not hurl innuendos. I admit it. It was part of my theatrical training: Impersonation in a hot climate.
RAMONA: You mean the gin was deliciously free. We can dispense with blackmail. It tends to become gray when

Act Two

played by both sides. We're going to use Plan B.
WOMAN *(Putting hand up to her heart)*: Plan B! Don't you think that's a little dangerous?
RAMONA: You might as well be hanged for a sheep as a lamb. Plan B will work. I'll double your salaries.
FIGURE: Triple them, and I'll agree.
WOMAN: I won't. I'd like a little slice of the pie. As I was saying . . .
RAMONA: All right. Four percent, divided between you.
WOMAN: That's better. [*WOMAN removes cape, puts on wig and eye glasses. FIGURE removes hood, puts on blond wig and dark glasses.*]
FIGURE: What am I supposed to do?
RAMONA: Stage effects. Smoke. The usual.
WOMAN: And me?
RAMONA: You'll be dressed to look exactly like Elena in her Marie Antoinette costume. The plan may take a few months. I'm going to get you into the house as servants. Meanwhile, there'll be refinements, strategies, costume fittings . . .
WOMAN: I could do it in my bare skin. David Belasco told me . . .
RAMONA: The lines have to be letter perfect. I'll say, "Did you leave a retainer for Ramona, Elena?" And *you* say, "The Russian Imperial Bonds in the folds of the green dress belong to Ramona." For credibility, add, "Baron Rothschild's doing very well." Got it?
WOMAN: O.K. You start.
RAMONA: "Did you leave a retainer for Ramona, Elena?"
WOMAN *(With theatrical gestures)*: "Did you leave a retainer for Ramona, Elena?"
RAMONA: What's the *matter* with you? That's my line. "The Russian Imperial Bonds . . ." Repeat.
WOMAN and FIGURE: The Russian Imperial Bonds repeat.
RAMONA: Take it again. Blah blah "retainer for Ramona,

Elena?"

WOMAN: And how is Baron Roth's *child* doing?

FIGURE: *Very* well.

RAMONA: Unless you creeps stop all this, I'm going to import someone competent from the Old Vic. Now this is your last . . . [*CORA enters.*]

CORA: Who are *they?*

RAMONA: The pantryman and the cook's helper from the agency.

CORA: They're quick. *(To RAMONA)* I suppose you've interviewed them?

RAMONA: They seem to know what they're about.

CORA *(To WOMAN)*: You understand I want somebody absolutely first rate.

WOMAN: I have trained abroad. I have cooked for royalty. Only my extraordinary modesty permits me to be an assistant.

CORA: Do you know how to make Milky Ways?

WOMAN *(Shocked)*: I do not make commercial candy, madame. I have an Order of Merit in molded aspics.

CORA: Oh. Well, aspics are just as good. As long as they're sweet. *(To FIGURE)* And you are an expert pantryman?

FIGURE: Queen Helwige de Holstein thought so.

CORA: Good. We're having our first trial buffet for sixty tonight at eight. *(By way of explanation)* A memorial buffet for my mother, the late Mrs. de Cordovan Barbridge.

WOMAN: The Speedy Gourmet Agency sends its condolences. As for my colleague and myself . . .

CORA: Thank you. We must go on with life, no matter the cost. *(Slight pause)* Which is what, by the way?

WOMAN: $350 a week, if I supply my own apron, or $350 a week if I don't.

CORA: At that salary, you don't need an apron. You can just trot down to Halston's . . .

RAMONA *(Quickly)*: She holds a Victoria Cross, madame, in chocolate pudding—Mr. Ashberry's favorite.

Act Two

CORA: Oh, all right. *(To FIGURE)* And you?
FIGURE: $400 a week, or $1750 a month, whichever is more or less.
CORA: Less. I want you both to stand behind the buffet and dole out.
WOMAN: That will be extra, madame.
CORA: But surely . . .
WOMAN: Madame. We would rather *starve* than haggle. Isn't that right, Bunny?
FIGURE: Madame does not seem to be familiar with the unwritten code of the kitchen.
RAMONA: Their recommendations are superb. *(Indicating WOMAN)* Mrs. Caronet has three diplomas in soufflés alone.
CORA: Well, in that case . . . *(Gritting her teeth)* Where excellence is involved, money is the second consideration. Pascal.
WOMAN: One question for the buffet: Does madame prefer "Selle d'Agneau Basquaise" or "Daube à l'Avignonnaise?"
CORA: I adore them both. *(Thinks. Lights up.)* I'll tell you what! I'll leave the whole thing in the hands of professionals! [*WOMAN curtsies, FIGURE bows as CORA exits rapidly.*]

CURTAIN

The Folding Green

ACT THREE

SCENE: *The living room. Three months later. A few changes have been made—a scarlet pillow on one chair, a yellow throw on the couch, a new painting, etc.*

AT RISE: *CORA is seated on the couch, holding two dresses in front of her. She examines them alternately.*

CORA: Cook! Cook! [*RAMONA enters in cook's uniform.*]
RAMONA: Yes, madame?
CORA: I want dinner to be something special tonight. The whole wolf pack's coming. Don't make something boring.
RAMONA: Has madame any suggestions?
CORA: Yes. An invitation to someone else's dinner.
RAMONA: Yes, madame.
CORA: Don't yes madame me, you half-baked cordon bleu. Make something gooey. Let them all drown in it!
RAMONA: Gooey ha-ha, or gooey elaborate?
CORA: And no more rice! Can't we have some meat?
RAMONA: Madame doesn't want to get beri-beri, does she?
CORA: At least it sounds edible. Don't you have any initiative? Pride in your work? Dream up something original, fresh . . .
RAMONA: Is that all, madame?
CORA: No, it isn't all. Stop trying to make my husband.
RAMONA: Madame!
CORA: Oh, don't play innocent. I saw you kiss him in the pantry.
RAMONA: Oh, no, madame!
CORA: Oh, yes, cook! And keep the mayonnaise out of everything. I'm sick of it.
RAMONA: But you always ask for something gooey!

Act Three

CORA: There are more gooey things on heaven and earth, Ramona, than are dreamt of in your philosophy.

RAMONA: Such as? I'd like to hear.

CORA: Whipped cream, sour cream, Bavarian cream . . .

RAMONA: Cream seems to be the extent of madame's repertoire, madame.

CORA: And marinate more. You don't marinate enough.

RAMONA: Marinate what, madame?

CORA: How should I know? I am the madame. You are the cook. And the ice cubes smell.

RAMONA: The ice cubes?

CORA: They have a rubbery smell. My martini last night was made of creosote practically.

RAMONA: But I do not make the drinks, madame. That is John's department.

CORA: You have a little excuse for everything, don't you? Stay away from my husband.

RAMONA: The situation is vice versa, madame. The gentleman is attempting to seduce me.

CORA: Not a very difficult project, I'd wager. Oh, get out! Sleep with him, sleep with everyone . . .

RAMONA: As you say, madame.

CORA: And don't mimic everything I say. *(Distractedly)* Why did I call you in?

RAMONA: The reunion.

CORA: Oh, yes. Last time the goose was greasy.

RAMONA: That is the goose's way, madame.

CORA: I do not have to be told the goose's way. We have the *Book of Knowledge* in the library. It is the cook's way to ungrease the goose.

RAMONA: I will do my best with an impossible task, madame.

CORA *(Pause)*: Where is my mother's book of epigrams? I want to say someting devastating at dinner.

RAMONA: You have used up the epigrams, madame. You will have to think for yourself this time. *(Aside to audience)*

The Folding Green

Speaking of impossible tasks.
CORA: Well, make one up for me. You're my Number One Girl.
RAMONA: No.
CORA *(Changing character, pleading)*: Ramona, please, just *one* epigram?
RAMONA: Oh, all right, just one. "They also wait who only stand and serve."
CORA: I don't get it.
RAMONA: It doesn't matter, as long as *they* get it. [*DONALD enters.*]
CORA: Donald dear, did you have a good golf?
DONALD: I lost my mashee in a water hole.
CORA: Is that good? Or bad?
DONALD: It was a tournament. There's no way of telling.
CORA: You look so tired, darling. *(To RAMONA)* That will be all. If your room is stifling, open a window. A happy servant makes a happy home.
RAMONA: The window's open and it's still stifling.
CORA: Then there's no solution, obviously. And let me compliment you on last night's chicken.
DONALD *(Casually slapping RAMONA on the behind)*: She's a real treasure, she is.
RAMONA: Thank you, *madman*. [*RAMONA exits.*]
DONALD: How was your day?
CORA: A miasma.
DONALD: Are we having the same road company tonight we had last night for dinner?
CORA: Last night we had two royalty, two distinguished, two physical beauty, two talented, and two money. Tonight is the reunion.
DONALD: They do come around fast, don't they? Well, we'll have all money for a change.
CORA: Did you try it again today?
DONALD: There's no use. The lawyers won't let me give another penny away. Something to do with taxes. And re-

Act Three

investing. And capital gains. They say the will is ironbound in every direction.

CORA: But how can it be? It was so confused.

DONALD: They fixed it up. We'll never be able to make another move without consulting fifty million experts.

CORA: Damn Elena! We're going mad with money—lawyers, brokers, lawsuits. Darling, can't we just go back to Cleveland? Can't we go back to being just incredibly rich?

DONALD: It's too late. And I have some bad news for you.

CORA: What?

DONALD: We own Patagonia.

CORA: But it took us a month to give Nicaragua away!

DONALD: I know. Another secret clause was opened yesterday. And, to top it off, India returned the smelting factory. Can't you shop more extravagantly?

CORA: There's nothing left to buy. The cellar is full of champagne and the attic is full of Picassos.

DONALD: How about some more servants?

CORA: Servants! We may be rich, but we're not *that* rich. Where would we find them?

DONALD: I don't know. Other people seem to have them.

CORA: But they're mostly relatives, aren't they?

DONALD: By the way, when I unloaded zinc this morning, the Bolivian cabinet fell.

CORA: I don't see the connection.

DONALD: Neither do I.

CORA: Buy zinc back.

DONALD: I did. And the Chilean cabinet fell.

CORA: The same old story. Every time we have a good dinner, another South American republic falls. It almost takes away one's appetite.

DONALD: Put a million dollars under everyone's plate tonight. That'll be something.

CORA: I don't think that would be in good taste. Besides, they don't want it any more than we do.

The Folding Green

DONALD: There must be *some* way out.
CORA: Can't we try throwing it away again?
DONALD: And be trailed all over Arizona by a hundred T-men, and that little girl from *Time Magazine* disguised as a dog?
CORA: I *know*. Well, let's get dressed. They'll be coming soon. [*Lights dim.*]
DONALD *(Advancing to footlights)*: Are you wearing your mink stole?
CORA *(Advancing to footlights)*: I'll be wearing my mink stole.
DONALD: You'll look chic in it again.
CORA: I'll look rich in it again. Are you wearing your black tie?
DONALD: I'll be wearing my black tie.
CORA: You'll be black and white again.
DONALD: I'll be black and white again. [*Lights dim.*]
CORA: I'm afraid in the dark . . .
DONALD: What *is* there in the dark?
CORA: There's an end in the dark.
DONALD: Yes, there's *that* in the dark.
CORA: When the sun goes down . . .
DONALD: Yes, I'm afraid *then* . . .
CORA: Shall we dress in the dark?
DONALD: No address in the dark.
CORA: Shall we dress?
DONALD: Yes.
[*Blackout. CORA and DONALD exit. The lights go up, but dimly. FIGURE and WOMAN enter from opposite sides of the stage. They meet as if in the middle of a battle scene, in a tremendous hurry.*]
FIGURE: The smoke pot broke down. I'm covered with soot.
WOMAN: Oh, God! Tonight of all nights!
FIGURE: I'm putting in a new wick. You brought the long matches?

Act Three

WOMAN *(Taking box of matches out from beneath her skirt)*: Here. Remember. From beneath the table, not from behind my skirt. I almost went up in flames at the rehearsal.
 FIGURE: You were two feet out of line. Stand back more. The table shaking device is in the oven. Take it out before the casserole goes in. Or we'll explode.
 WOMAN: Where's the other wig?
 FIGURE: In the freezer. Behind the Stouffer Welsh Rarebit.
 WOMAN: First, flames. Now, the freezer. What do you want me to get—pneumonia?
 FIGURE: "Some say the world will end in fire,/ Some say in ice . . ."
 WOMAN: *Very* funny.
 FIGURE: Slip the wig into the oven when the casserole comes out. It'll warm up in no time.
 WOMAN: Hot, wet hair—just what I've always wanted.
 FIGURE: You're getting edgy. Calm down. Everything's going according to plan.
 WOMAN: I must be gaining weight. The Marie Antoinette skirt hardly goes around any more. And I have to keep the hors d'oeuvres hidden in it until the very last moment!
 FIGURE: Your room in fifteen minutes?
 WOMAN *(Looks at watch)*: Twelve. Synchronize.
 FIGURE *(Adjusting his watch)*: Right. Twelve it is. *(On the way out)* Ciao.
 WOMAN *(Looking after him)*: Don't mention food to *me*.
 [*WOMAN exits. Sound of a door bell. Then, full lights up. LAWRENCE, TERESA and FELICITY enter. FELICITY has a new blond wig and is very sleek. TERESA and LAW-RENCE treat each other with almost open contempt. Married, and having found each other out, they are beginning to dislike each other publicly.*]
 TERESA: A Sultan's welcome as usual. We're not even announced by the butler.
 FELICITY: I think he died. Or was a victim of automation, or something.

The Folding Green

TERESA *(To LAWRENCE)*: Ever since I married you, they've been treating us shabbily. Whose stupid idea was it to have these monthly reunions?
LAWRENCE: Yours.
TERESA: Then, why bring it up?
LAWRENCE: Because you asked me to, that's why.
TERESA: This room still looks like an archeological dig.
FELICITY: How I dread this! The tediousness of it!
LAWRENCE: We all know each other too well. Everything came out during the hearing . . . Who slept with whom, who tried to cheat whom . . .
TERESA: That was *every*body, wasn't it?
FELICITY: Well, the hearing's behind us, and we're all filthy rich. The trouble is we never settle anything. Can't we ever settle anything? *(To LAWRENCE)* Make us some drinks darling, will you?
LAWRENCE: The usual?
TERESA: Curare on the rocks for me. [*LAWRENCE makes drinks.*]
FELICITY: I'm really quite beside myself. I sold my aluminum shares to buy a dog, and there was a wave of suicides on Wall Street.
LAWRENCE: The dog must have been mammoth.
FELICITY: It was. The lawyers made me give it back, and it bit one of them so hard, they had to dissolve the firm.
TERESA: Serves those shysters right. [*LAWRENCE serves the drinks. No one thanks him.*]
LAWRENCE *(Drinking)*: Thank you, Lawrence Hawley, for making the drinks. Thank *you*, Lawrence Hawley . . .
TERESA: Oh, don't be more of a bore than you are. Sit down . . . and . . . take your pulse.
LAWRENCE: Do you think it could possibly be as dull this time as last?
FELICITY: I most certainly do.
LAWRENCE: Reunions! How can you reunite what never was united?

Act Three

TERESA: What distaste tears apart convenience glues together.

LAWRENCE: Maybe something interesting has happened to Cora and Donald.

TERESA: Nothing very interesting happens to people with money. That's what the money's for, to prevent it.

FELICITY: Elena was interesting. I'll say that for her.

TERESA: The only thing interesting that's happened to me is getting married. It's forced me to find stimulation elsewhere. [CORA and DONALD enter.]

CORA: Darlings! I'm so glad to see you all. *(Stares at FELICITY.)* Who's *that?*

FELICITY: It's me, Felicity!

CORA *(Kissing her on cheek)*: I didn't recognize you. You look . . . solved.

DONALD: You haven't been waiting long, have you?

TERESA: Just an eternity. We exhausted general topics.

CORA: There are few things that can be exhausted as quickly.

FELICITY: Agriculture is another.

LAWRENCE: I find life terribly dull without Elena.

TERESA: That's all he talks about: Elena, Elena, Elena.

DONALD: And how are we going to get rid of her money? I wake up every day with the shudders. More tax forms, more sessions with her lawyers, more cables from Europe, more oil wells gushing their heads off. All I wanted to do was live comfortably. But this, this is *too* much.

TERESA: The only thing to do, really, is to stop production. I mean everywhere. And they won't let us do that. People would starve.

CORA: How did Elena manage it all? I had no idea, did you, that she was running the world?

TERESA: *I* did. I just didn't realize how God damn big the world is.

LAWRENCE: If I knew then what I know now, I would have holed up in a cold-water flat forever.

The Folding Green

TERESA: And stayed a bachelor, I presume.
LAWRENCE: Or at least married a representational painter.
TERESA *(Putting her hands on table)*: Elena's money is a curse. We should never . . . [*The table shakes, smoke, etc.*] Look! The table's moving! [*Lights up. WOMAN, dressed in Marie Antoinette costume, is standing next to table.*]
FELICITY: Elena!
[*FELICITY has only two more lines in this play. From here on in, she starts a kind of elaborate vaudeville act in pantomime. She drinks steadily, fades in and out of the action, comments mutely on a particular speech by a grimace, a motion of her hands, an imitation. Sometimes she simply lies down on a couch and is ignored. This should all be deadpan and understated. RAMONA enters.*]
RAMONA *(To CORA)*: Did you ring, madame?
WOMAN: Good evening, Ramona.
RAMONA *(Turning around, as if suddenly aware of her)*: My God! Elena!
WOMAN *(To RAMONA)*: Ask me the question nearest your heart, my dear. Is there any little request you would like to make to the gods?
RAMONA: I'm flabbergasted! *(To others)* It's Elena!
CORA: We have eyes.
WOMAN: Any little request at all.
RAMONA: Well . . . did you leave a retainer for Ramona, Elena? [*Table shakes, smoke, etc. When it clears, ELENA, wearing Marie Antoinette costume, is standing at other end of table from WOMAN.*]
LAWRENCE: I think I'm getting double vision.
WOMAN *(Panicky)*: The Russian Imperial . . . *(Puts hands to head.)* God, it's cold in here!
DONALD: What the hell's going on?
ELENA: I was heading for the Isle of Wight and look where I am! Home!
WOMAN *(Desperately, looking at RAMONA)*: Baron Rothschild's doing very well. [*A puff of smoke from beneath the*

Act Three

table]
RAMONA: Stop it, you idiot!
CORA *(To RAMONA)*: Whom are you talking to?
RAMONA: To myself. I'm nervous. Aren't *you*?
ELENA: And what a trip! I had to fly *below* the weather!
DONALD: I think we should call someone.
CORA: Who do you suggest? The FBI or the Chase Manhattan Bank?
TERESA: You don't think they could possibly be twins?
WOMAN *(To ELENA)*: You fake! What are you doing wearing my costume?
ELENA *(To WOMAN)*: The shoe is on the other foot, my dear. Your slip is showing and your wig is dripping.
WOMAN: My slip? . . . *(Surveys herself.)*
ELENA *(Hard)*: Who *are* you?
WOMAN *(To RAMONA)*: Who *am* I?
RAMONA: Don't ask me. I have enough trouble keeping track of who I am.
WOMAN: We rise above identity in the spirit world. Now I am myself. I *was* Elena.
ELENA: Was you, Minnie?
LAWRENCE: I don't believe in the spirit world. What sort of racket are you girls involved in?
CORA: No. I think one of them is real. I mean in a spirit way . . .
ELENA: Minnie, are you real?
RAMONA: Do you smell something burning? In the kitchen? Excuse me . . .
ELENA: Stay where you are. [RAMONA, *frightened, complies.*]
TERESA: Are you dead or alive? *(To ELENA)* I mean you.
ELENA: What a question! I'm here.
CORA: Let's stop all this mucking about. *(To ELENA)* Who exactly are you?
ELENA: I'm Elena, of course.

TERESA: But *I* went to the cremation!
LAWRENCE: I used to be able to tell the living from the dead . . .
ELENA: You were fortunate.
CORA: And now you've come down from . . . from . . .
ELENA: Clouds. Vapors. Air. Space, mysterious space.
CORA *(To WOMAN)*: And you?
WOMAN: *I* am Elena. She's an imposter. I should think my own daughter would know me.
CORA: Then answer two questions: Why did you leave the money in green things that fold? And why are you wearing that dress?
WOMAN: Capriciousness is a garden. Everything that grows unfolds in green. And I am wearing this costume because I died in it. Even the dead have sentimental attachments.
ELENA: Now let me ask you a few salient questions. Did the Baron de Cordovan have a mustache?
WOMAN: I won't be subjected . . .
ELENA: Answer it straight.
WOMAN: The gods will be angry. I bring an important message . . .
LAWRENCE: Go on. Answer it.
WOMAN: He had . . . a sort of disputable grayish-black, sometimes tan fuzz . . .
ELENA: A description scientific in the extreme. Did the late Mr. Barbridge sport a Van Dyke?
WOMAN: What an ugly use of the word "sport." Really!
ELENA: Did he?
RAMONA *(Unable to control herself)*: Yes, he did!
FELICITY: She's coaching her!
WOMAN: There are Van Dykes and Van Dykes.
ELENA: And there are Hals and Hals.
WOMAN: I, er . . . it was so long ago . . .
[*There is a tremendous burst of smoke. Stage is obscured for a moment. A slight scream is heard on the word "Bunny!" When the smoke clears, WOMAN is gone.*]

Act Three

RAMONA: The pyrotechnics of heaven!
FELICITY *(Calling to wings)*: Elena! Elena!
ELENA: Yes, my dear?
FELICITY: If you're Elena, who was she?
ELENA: Ask Ramona.
RAMONA: I haven't the faintest . . .
ELENA: You hired her, didn't you?
RAMONA: Absurd! I've been cooking all day. I know nothing about it.
ELENA: You *are* the fool! Don't you understand I was trying to find out whom *not* to leave the money to? I chose you. I made a mistake.
RAMONA: *Not* to leave the money? *You're* the fool. Who wants to be spared a bequest?
ELENA: People who can live without them.
RAMONA: It's easy for you to talk. Up to your elbows in cash!
ELENA: Every inheritance is a potential sinking fund. *(To all)* I once had your combined incomes. Did you ever hear me complain? I did what I liked because I knew what I liked; I went where I went because I knew where to go. But you! *(To RAMONA)* Look at them.
RAMONA: I'm looking.
ELENA: And what do you see?
RAMONA: Money. Lovely money. What do *you* see?
ELENA: An untrained chorus about to sing, "Onward Christian Golfers."
RAMONA: It's grand to be eccentric. The poor can't afford it.
DONALD *(To ELENA)*: Let me understand you. You don't think money is important?
ELENA: Money is very important. It shows us what happiness is by not being it.
TERESA: I'd rather be unhappy *with* it.
ELENA: You are. Your wish has been granted.

The Folding Green

RAMONA: And you had some crazy idea money wouldn't make me happy?
ELENA: Yes, I did. I always thought you were more intelligent than you did.
RAMONA: I stand in front of a stove all day. That doesn't seem nearly as good to me as going to Venice.
ELENA: Venice is full of stoves.
RAMONA: And canals. I wouldn't expect to be cooking in Venice.
ELENA: Ah, but *someone* is. Someone happier or less happy than you. Someone you'll never meet, riding on your canal.
RAMONA: I'm not going to Venice, alas. Thanks to you.
ELENA: I don't owe you anything. But you'll be going to Venice.
CORA: She'll get no recommendation from me!
ELENA: That might make it easier for her. *(To RAMONA)* Since you do not know how to be free, I think you should be rich. The Russian Imperial Bonds in the folds of the green dress belong to Ramona.
RAMONA *(To herself)*: The plan's working!
CORA: The bonds are mine. I've already reinvested them—it's too late.
ELENA: No. Yours are yours and hers are hers.
CORA: Sharing my inheritance with a servant!
ELENA: You're not sharing it. There's plenty to go around. *(To all)* And I have been dreadfully misunderstood. I'm not the sort of person who would leave the same thing to two people.
CORA: What a mother you've been! Selfish, arrogant . . .
ELENA *(To CORA)*: When you get to the point, why don't you strike a gong . . . in case I've dozed off.
RAMONA: Money . . . the end of drudgery.
ELENA: You are rich, my dear. Now you can be your own companion. Like these wretched creatures.
RAMONA: I might as well be my own companion as yours.

Act Three

ELENA: Perhaps. I hope you won't be lonely.

DONALD: And who was that other woman? A companion's companion's companion?

RAMONA: I hired her. I wanted what belonged to me. I arranged the seance—at least the phoney part of it.

CORA: When I think I could have thrown you out . . .

ELENA: You're losing nothing but an incompetent cook.

LAWRENCE: Elena, but why choose Ramona? What made her so special?

ELENA: Her shorthand *does* have the quality of illuminated manuscripts and she *does* have extrasensory perception. Is there anyone here who can say as much? And she was my companion for twenty-five years, the person I saw.

CORA: And you think that's such a great distinction?

ELENA: It was a great distinction to me.

CORA: I could never tell you this when you were alive, but I can tell you now. A lot of people think you're nuts.

ELENA: You've mixed your tenses, as usual. I thought of other people's opinions a great deal, while you were perfecting your golf game in Cleveland. And the answer was simple: A lot of people will think a lot of things. Unfortunately, most of them are only happy when they come to the same conclusions. *(To CORA, with compassion, not condescension or spite)* Thought has escaped you, my dear. You are sensationally lucky.

TERESA: That's my definition of luck: no brains and lots of money.

WOMAN *(Entering as cook's assistant)*: The muffin's have collapsed! *(To RAMONA)* Hurry! *(Turning)* Why it's Mrs. Barbridge! Nice to see you, ma'am.

ELENA: How do you do.

RAMONA: I'm going to Venice.

WOMAN: And I'm going to scream. *(She screams.)* Now I'll tell you the real truth. The muffins have not only collapsed—they're growing in the inverse direction.

RAMONA: Oh, all right. One last gasp for Old Gourmet.

The Folding Green

[*WOMAN and RAMONA exit.*]
ELENA: The room is cleared of assistants. [*There is total silence. ELENA breaks it the way a person conscious of a lull in conversation relieves other people of responsibility.*] Well, here you are, looking like deserted children. *Rich* deserted children. I hope you're all satisfied, now that you have everything you wanted . . . town houses, tea houses, publishing houses, summer houses . . . *(Pause)* You'd be surprised how the value of silence increases with age.

CORA: Then why do you talk so much?

ELENA: That's how I keep the silence going.

LAWRENCE *(First human remark)*: How are you, Elena?

ELENA: I get a bit disoriented when I make the journey down these days.

DONALD: You mean you've been down before?

ELENA: Oh, yes. I sat through the entire hearing when you all defamed each other. I enjoyed it immensely. I was that seedy little gamin in tweeds in the third row. *(Pause)* I should have flown a little harder. You all look old. You don't even know how to pamper yourselves.

TERESA: We have too much money, Elena.

ELENA: Throw it away then. What difference does it make?

DONALD: That's easier said than done. You can't throw factories away. You can't stop oil from coming up from the earth.

CORA: Our lives have become virtual banking operations. We're miserable.

ELENA: Well, then, the only thing left to do, obviously, is to die. I'm quite happy.

TERESA: But you're securely in heaven, aren't you?

ELENA: Of course. Hell is a one-way ticket.

DONALD: How do we know we'll get in?

ELENA: As a matter of fact, most of you won't. I haven't allowed a bore in for three months. I see no reason to make exceptions for relatives. I've given you every material oppor-

Act Three

tunity to be happy. I don't see why I should concern myself with you further.

CORA: I wouldn't play that note, if I were you. Your will was such a mess we had to hire seventeen lawyers to straighten it out. It was only then we hit on the device of dividing it equally.

ELENA: Such is the folly of human greed. You have my money; now you want my brains. *They*'re nonnegotiable.

CORA: Perhaps we could do something *good* with the money?

ELENA: There is nothing as despicable as inertia disguised as a moral scruple. You have to know what *good* is, first. It is too late to mourn the fact that the human body can only wear one set of clothes at a time, the mouth ingest so much food, the skin take in so much sun. Stew in your own juice; it's a very expensive concoction.

DONALD: And you won't help us?

ELENA: I can only help you by showing you that you need no help. You have everything people want when they want everything.

TERESA: And you won't take back some of the money?

ELENA: There are no pocketbooks in heaven.

CORA *(Pitifully)*: We own Patagonia.

ELENA: Good. The swimming on the coast is justly celebrated.

CORA: I sit in the living room day after day, smoking. I think: I could do this, I could do that. Oh, I used to go to lectures and things, after there was nothing to shop for. I have nothing to do.

ELENA: Learn French and read French literature from the beginning. After that, there's German, Russian, Urdu, Zulu . . .

DONALD: I didn't know Zulus wrote.

ELENA: It surprises me to hear you say that. I've saved your letters.

CORA: Is that all the advice you have for me, Elena?

127

The Folding Green

Languages?
ELENA: Have a child, stupid.
TERESA: You have a new serenity, Elena. I wish I knew the secret.
ELENA: Any open window will do.
CORA: But how do you *really* occupy your time?
ELENA: Machiavelli runs an amusing little seminar.
TERESA: My idea of heaven is so vague . . .
ELENA: Since heaven, like everything else, is a product of the mind, I *think*.
DONALD: But everyone says . . .
ELENA: Fools tell fools. The kindest fool is not tolerated in paradise. Whatever you hear to the contrary is false. Purgatory was created for the merely nice and the halfwit; it is neither here nor there, and it looks astonishingly like this room.
DONALD: Let's get back to money. What are we going to do?
ELENA: This is my last advice to you: become intelligent or die.
CORA: And the money?
ELENA *(Getting bored)*: I must go.
CORA: You're not staying for dinner?
ELENA: Alas, no. I have an appointment on the Isle of Wight. Tomorrow morning, a miraculous birth will be announced in the newspapers.
LAWRENCE: A miraculous birth?
ELENA: Like any other. *(Lights dim.)* Greetings from the dead. Goodnight, goodnight.
[*Lights out. ELENA exits.*]
VOICES: Elena, where are you? She's gone! Put the lights on! [*Lights go on.*]
DONALD: I'm going back to Cleveland.
TERESA: And I'm going to paint again.
LAWRENCE: Don't be silly. All of you . . . you can't be what you were. It's too late.

Act Three

CORA: You only say that because you were never anybody.

LAWRENCE: None of us ever were. I seem to be the only person who knows it.

DONALD: Well, we can finish discussing this at dinner. [*THEY all rise.*]

LAWRENCE: Let's have a toast. [*ALL lift glasses.*] To Elena. Our benefactor.

TERESA: Benefactor! [*TERESA begins to laugh. As RAMONA enters, she stops abruptly.*]

RAMONA: The last supper is done. We're skipping one course. The shrimp wouldn't come out of their shells. [*RAMONA exits. The phone rings.*]

CORA *(Answering)*: Hello. Elena! Hello, hello . . . *(SHE listens, hangs up slowly.)* That was Elena. She said she forgot to tell us the most important cliché of all. Love is the secret of happiness.

TERESA: Oh? Do you think it really is?

CORA *(Half mocking, half believing)*: It must be. We've tried everything else. [*JOHN appears at dining-room doors.*]

JOHN: Dinner, such as it was, is served.

CORA: In you go, pets. *(After a slight pause)* "They also wait who only stand and serve."

TERESA *(No enthusiasm)*: Devastating!

[*They file in. JOHN shuts doors. As they shut, RAMONA enters and seats herself at the original table used in Act I.*]

RAMONA *(Writing in her stenographer's notebook)*: Dinner, February 8, 1963*: Bon Ami Cocktail with Detergent Sauce, Brooms Bourguignon, Potatoes Comet and Ajax . . . [*ELENA enters and sits down opposite RAMONA.*]

ELENA: I'd hate to try your meatloaf. It seems incredible that they're still alive.

RAMONA: I know. They must be made of iron.

ELENA *(Change of tone)*: How *are* you, Ramona?

---

*This date should always be that of the particular production.

The Folding Green

RAMONA: Fine. And bored. I've cooked everything in the house. Even the lamps. They didn't even miss them. I suppose you're *dining*, these days?
ELENA: Yes. The dead dine.
RAMONA: Do you ever see Freddie? Does he ask for me?
ELENA: He told me to give you his regards.
RAMONA: Sweet. Tell me something, Elena, what's this play all about?
ELENA: The subject is money.
RAMONA: And the theme?
ELENA: An attack on the rational.
RAMONA: And that's all?
ELENA: The play makes a last stand for the lost art of the epigram.
RAMONA: I see. But what about the actors and the spirits? Supposing we got through to them tonight. How would we know which is which?
ELENA: Ah, my dear, that is something we will never know. [*Curtain begins to descend very slowly. ELENA looking up and noticing it, puts her hand out toward it.*] Stop! [*The curtain stops. ELENA turns to RAMONA, and in a gesture of courtesy as well as urgency, a kind of sitting bow, she must communicate to the audience her awareness that there is still a line to come, still some unfinished business that must be accomplished before the curtain finally falls.*]
RAMONA (*Thinks. Then slowly*): I hear this play is folding...
[*As soon as RAMONA says this, the lighting on the stage turns green. ELENA and RAMONA in tableau for a second.*]

CURTAIN

HOWARD MOSS

Howard Moss is the poetry editor of *The New Yorker*. Before joining its staff in 1948, he was an instructor of English at Vassar College. The author of ten books of poems and two books of criticism, *The Magic Lantern of Marcel Proust* and *Writing Against Time*, he has also edited the poems of Keats, the nonsense verse of Edward Lear, a collection of short stories written by poets, *The Poet's Story*, and a collection of poems entitled *New York: Poems*. In 1972 Moss received the National Book Award for his *Selected Poems*.

PS 3525 .O8638 T85 1980x

Moss, Howard, 1922-

Two plays by Howard Moss.